How I made $2,000 Winning Free Demo Trading Contests (forex and binary options)
- Teemy

Watch Videos

Download Videos

Download Tools

Download Volume Allocator

Dedication & Appreciation

Dedicated to the folks at forexfactory thread <u>Verbal diarrhea matches trading skills?</u>
Who made a procrastinator dust up his boots.

Table of Contents

Chapter 1	-	General Introduction to Trading Contests
1.1	-	Brief Overview
1.2	-	About Me
1.3	-	How To Win – Rules
1.4	-	Lite Forex Contests
Chapter 2	-	InstaForex Contests
Chapter 3	-	More Contests
3.1	-	Alpari Virtual Reality
3.2	-	Extra Contests
Chapter 4	-	Doing the Math
Chapter 5	-	How To Win – Strategy
Chapter 6	-	My Tools
Chapter 7	-	Bonus Lecture
7.1	-	In Closing
7.2	-	One for the Road

Chapter 1 - General Introduction to Trading Contests

1,1 (Brief Overview)

I will be taking you through the Table of Contents.

Introduction: We'll be talking about forex contests in general and you'll be meeting me here and I will be talking about contests I've won so far in the past and then now we'll talk about how you can also duplicate such just by following some of the methods I used.

There are some tools that actually make your trading better and then a bit of extra information you might need.

- Types of trading contests
- Profitability and the prizes being won
- Who organizes the contests?
- Why organize contests?
- Where are they listed?
- Types of trading contests

There are various types of contests being organized on various brokerages. Some are demo and some are live contests. In the demo contests, you really don't need to put any money in it. The broker just opens an account for you with prefunded funds and then you just trade and win.

And the live contest, you actually have to put in your own money and the prizes on demo compared to the live they are quite different that is because people are actually risking money on real and they get to make a lot more compared to that of demo.

I also think some also organize raffle contests I would say and these ones it is just a matter of make a deposit into an account and then a raffle will be organized and one person just wins. Just a lucky dip and sometimes it could even be promotion contests like "who can give us the largest number of new referrals?"

Alright let's talk about contests and their prizes.

Here we have Tickmill giving out gold bars for prize.

InstaForex offering cars. They actually love giving out cars anyway and of course they do give out trading credits.

Another broker that also loves giving out cars and also electronic gadgets; iPhone, iPad, and even cars: OctaFX.

The One Million Dollar contest by XM markets. That was last year (2017) and the finals took place live in Thailand. It wasn't an hidden event. These are the lucky winners it was shown live on TV and even on the internet. A million dollars contest.

- Profitability of contests: We've talked about that.

- Who organized contests? Why organize contests?

So mainly we are brokers that organize contests and it's usually because of publicity.

Next we also have Financial Institutions who actually organize contests to school universities and so on or even just any corporate trading body who want to find out new traders for the future of the company, let me put it that way.

Scouting Agencies do it for commissions so they a finish can feed all these financial institutions and then, we also have Philanthropists just a matter of giving back to the society.

Brokers have been doing these promotions all this whie. Giving out free demo accounts or they give higher leverages or give you opening bonus. More recently contests and we have lots of brokers now running contests.

Where are they listed?

You can take a google search for "forex contests list" or "forex competitions list" and then you would have a large volume. Some are actually aggregators that combine all these contests together and into one place.

100ForexBrokers.com, that is their page here. BestForexBonus.com, here is the link. MyFxBook.com also and CashBackFx.com.

Okay, I plan on doing that also in the future and I also want to do it a little bit better than the way these guys have been running it but actually, they've been doing a good job so far.

1,2 (About Me)

Okay, here I am this is me and that's my website which I've been building for the past ten years amongst others. My name is Temitayo Akinrinola but online you are actually meeting me as Teemy.

So, this is what I do. I'm actually a programmer, I'm a marketer, well actually this is my first real product that I'm actually marketing and I'm also a trader. A programmer in the HTML, PHP and Metatrader4 programming languages and I trade currencies and a little bit of binary.

Do you remember this book then by Nicholas Darvas? I don't think it was actually written by him but this is the book that actually talked about " How I Made 2 Million From The Stock Market". So, I actually thought about... well, that wasn't my initial plan actually.

It was part of a bigger plan, a bigger book of like 20-something chapters and all of a sudden I decided to just subtract one of these chapters to write something out because it's been taking just too long for me to just bring out the whole thing, so i decided to just write out of the book "How I made $2,000 Winning Free Demo Trading Contests" following the same format Nicholas Darvas used in his book, the story about how he got to achieve that feat so I decided to just follow the same format without having to just think too much. It wasn't hard to do anyway because it's something I actually did in reality.

Alright, these are the contests I actually won in the past and these are the prizes I won from each of them. I'll be talking about each of these contests and that's what we'll be using majorly for the greater part of this book. How to win these kinds of contests in similar fashion.

Now, 1st place, LiteForex Master Demo Competition which actually is no more running. I got first prize of $100. Actually I wasn't on number one at that time, I was in number 3 but the first two people were disqualified. I don't know and I got first place and that's the prize I won.

InstaForex 1st place Million Option Demo Contest. I'got first place I made $500 and the highest I got then was around 310 or 340 points/ Don't worry, we'll see that in action later.

And then the LiteForex Fighting Demo. It's also not running anymore I won that in 2012, rather, I won 4th place in 2012 and this same contest I also repeated in the winning here, 2nd place here.

And this same Million Option, I got 4th place for a prize of $200. Actually I wasn't even 4th at that time, I think I was also 8th. I was propped up to number 4. So actually, people do get disqualified. You will also be learning why and how people get disqualified and how to avoid that happening to you.

Then same LiteForex Top10 Demo competition which is the same as.... okay Top10 is different from Fighting, I came out number 10 position, $10. Quite good.

And InstaForex Great Race, that was like a one month contest. I will tell you the duration of the other ones later on when we get to breaking down on how to win them. So, I won $400 for sixth place.

InstaForex FX1 Demo contest which is a one-day contest Rally. I made $400, first prize is actually $500.

And then the LiteForex Top10 Demo trading contest, I came out 1st and I remember this was a very fantastic contest. From $10,000 to $3m in a period of five days, actually it was a week contest.

And then, the Alpari contest here which I won last year was just 1000 Alpari points and at (error statement) a hundred being equal to $1 so 1000 give me ten dollars actually.

And then, 2nd place in InstaForex Sniper which was last year. This is $400 and so far so good, I haven't won any one this year. I actually could have gotten something that was last week but I messed it up. I will tell you how how and how you can also avoid it too.

Alright, so far so good, those are the contests I've won and then we'll now talk about how you can actually go ahead to win them, everything about them, the breakdown about the contest in general, the prizes a you could have won if you were in 1st place and at least come out of the contest with a prize anytime you go ahead into taking them.

There is no guarantee that you will win everything or even anything for that matter but the thing is if you keep trying, you will get something at the end of the day. So the plan is to get the first, you plan towards getting the first that's what this training is about. Think about how you can get the first but whatever you get, even if it is just like you say "shoot for the moon and land among the stars" something like that, right. So we'll aim towards getting you the first position but if you can't at least you you'll get a prize and the prize at least whatever it is you might have paid for this book, it definitely would cover up for it comparing to all these by far. You can even still be doing all this over and over and remember these are all demo contests. It doesn't cost you any money at all and it's all free.

1.3 (How To Win – Rules)

- Registration, Start Dates & Duration

Now, The major things we have to take note about when you are going to win any context is, consider the rules and also consider the strategies you are going to use. Sometimes the rules determine the strategies you end up using.

Alright, so we have the registrations and the start dates and the duration, some contests allow you to register ahead of the contest and the registration date lapses till the very end of the contest while some let their registration dates end BEFORE the contest starts and then the contest starts until the end and you can't even register thereafter.

You have to take care of those registration dates and so the first thing you have to do is immediately you see a contest is available, register for it don't postpone it till a future date because you might end up forgetting when you are so busy with everything about life and so on and all of a sudden, it's time for the contest but you haven't registered and you can't actually do anything at that point so the first thing, any time you have a chance when you see a contest, register for it keep the details somewhere and any time the contest starts, you go along with it.

- The Volume of Traders:

Some are open-ended and some are closed-ended. Some allow as many traders as possible - which is what most do anyways - allow as many traders as possible to register to enter into their contest while some allow only a limited number of traders into their contest, maybe like when a particular number is achieved, then they stop the contest registration*.

- Then, The Winner Rankings:

Almost all the brokers have a section on their page whereby we have this listing, leaderboard to see which position everybody is but the thing you can actually get too engrossed with checking out the leader ranking, you might end up making a mistake and sometimes if you look at it, it can actually help you know whether to do better or to just slow down and so on so you have to be careful to know what it is used for there.

- Cheating and Disqualification:

Sometimes you might even do something that you don't think actually is against the rule but until you actually go through the rules for you to know that. So it's always good to always take a look at the rules and what the broker will see as not being fair play because they are actually against people cheating. In the rules it's all described so take a look at the rules and to avoid disqualification.

After winning, even some rules still apply till after you've won the contest because some brokers don't allow you to use their contest to promote yourself and say "hey I won this contest"! Some don't allow you to do that and then you have to be careful about how you do your money because I've wasted a lot of this money in the past you know. You win a contest, you're happy and then before you know it pium* the next day or the next week you've already blown up the whole account.

So if it's actually part of you what you've been doing before… you've been blowing accounts before you won a contest. So when you win a contest, you will most likely end up blowing the account as well if you don't change your ways let me put it that way. So, you have to have a calm mind, a cool head before you before you start working on the winnings anyways.

- And the strategy you will be using:

So I'll be using the ones I won to actually explain the strategies you use for each of these contests. As I said earlier, we'll be talking about your planning and strategy which is usually determined by the rules and the rules is different from one contest to the other.

Your trading system which you use and some funny or let me say special strategies you can actually use but you may or may not use them depending on the rules and then some tools which actually I use and some I will actually let you know what they are.

So, I was able to break down all of these into these special collections. These are the LiteForex contests. These are the InstaForex contests and this at last the Alpari contest.

So we will start with the InstaForex contests… sorry the LiteForex contests.

1,4 (Lite Forex Contests)

LiteForex Index Master contest used to run a long time ago because it's no more running right now. I will still explain all the same because that's what I promised you. Alright so, Index Master is a forex trading contest that involves LiteForex Indices*. I mean it's just a matter of packing all the currencies together and trying to bring out let's say the strength of each particular currency.

Let me explain that now.

Alright here is a chart showing all the various currencies. The currency instruments on the LiteForex Index contest then. We are having EURLFX (LiteForexIndex) then GBPLFX, CADLFX, NZDLF except in the case of the JPY where we have LFXJPY. These are all of those currencies more like showing the strength. There is a formula which is actually used to calculate all these price values. Its actually a CFD or let's say a derivative just extracted and brought out just for people to just trade specifically on LiteForex, so you won't see it on any other brokerage. More like also showing the strength of each currency.

They are actually meant for let's say for instance you want to trade EURUSD or should you trade EURJPY, you are not sure which is which but you are sure that the Euro is strong. So, what about just go ahead and trade on the EURLFX.

That's why the derivative was actually created. So, we will get people now introduced to it and let people be used to trading it so they actually involved a… they created a contest which is the LiteForex Index so traders could actually get introduced to their derivatives. So, that's why the contest came up; the LiteForex Index Master contest and I won it once… won 1st once I think. Yeah.

This is what it is.

The charts are still there so you can actually go ahead and trade the contest* but that's not possible anyway because that's a matter of the past now. Because people actually use… people have gotten to know about it unless they reintroduce the contest before you can say you can get to see it again.

So, about winning it now, each of these currencies has gotten its own average daily movement. Let me put each of them on the H1 chart. So, you can actually trade any one of them but some will actually give you much more returns than the others. Then we usually used to rush ahead and trade the LFXJPY then but the spread was actually higher, much higher. I think it was like 35 pips or so compared to these other guys that were like 10 pips thereabout.

So, know how to balance it out based on what the spread of each one would be. But it is something in the past, you can't get the full rules, I can't really say so much about it right now but the thing is that this is just the LiteForex Index once again and if you feel like trading it as a trader on LiteForex, yes you can go ahead and during the contest it is just a matter of… I think the highest prize… the highest amount, we started from $10,000 and take it down to as high as you could then.

I think the highest amount then was around 70*-something thousand dollars. So, if you take it from $10,000 to around 70-something thousand dollars, you have a good chance of making 1st, 2nd or 3rd but mostly you can actually get the first position there. So, from 10,000* to 70-

something thousand... 70+ thousand, you can actually get a good ranking on LiteForex Index back then.

One more... so , I said for the LiteForex Index from 10k to around 70+k. That was what guaranteed a win then. One more thing about the rules is that LiteForex Index actually had a lot more than these eight pairs initially. We had like the DAX index and several other indices* like that but after a while, the rules were changed and it was limited to just these guys (hope I am accurate*).

So, as I said earlier on, the rules dictate the strategy you use. So when later it was just these guys then... it was just these guys as it were. Alright so, there we go.

Now that we are coming to the next contest which is the LiteForex Fighting Competition. Okay, now it seems that I actually made a mistake. This is what should have been here and this was around 30-something k... 33k. Let's say around... let me delete this okay. This was actually from 10k to around 70k thereabout that would guarantee a win there. This was supposed to be 33 sorry, my bad.

Alright, so LiteForex Fighting was just a contest that involves normal LiteForex currencies or any one you so desire and just go ahead and just win but it was a 1-day contest. Index was a 1-week* contest, no, it was a 1-day contest on Monday and LiteForex Fighting was a 1-day contest on Wednesday. So, you have to just start with $10,000 and you have to make it to as any amount that you can. There are really... there was practically no rules in this case. If you can get the maximum balance you could so if you could raise an account from 10k to 70k which is something many traders were able to do.

Back then I think I wasn't... the highest I was able to achieve on that one was just... the fighting, the highest I was able to get was just 4th place and so far so good though it's still okay anyway. But the thing is it was actually a highly competitive contest because you have to be at a really... let me say on a favorable day for you for you to actually be able to achieve this.

It's not just about you being a good trader but also about your system aligns on that particular day for a particular currency. Waiting for another currency, waiting for another currency, waiting for another currency and before you know it, the whole day is gone. Alright, you just have to like…just be on your luck day. I really hate to use the word luck but that's just it. Go ahead and just win the contest.

LiteForexTop10 is similar to the Fighting contest but it was a 1-week contest. This is one of my favorites because you actually have a period of one week to go ahead to start your… it starts with 10k, a one week to actually trade the contest. You actually could have enough time to win here and so you could keep on balancing until the whole one week is expired and then you can actually have something to show unlike one that you have to... well, a whole lot of... let's say you don't really have enough time to actually get to be balanced enough to do everything that you wanted to achieve within that one day but if you have a full one week of trading, yes you can actually achieve much a lot more and be much more balanced and settle the whole thing out.

So you start with 10k now. Now, this contest is such that if you can actually go ahead and make it towards 320k in a week, you can actually make 1st or 2nd or 3rd. This is how it goes.

Let's say first day 10k to 20k and the second day 20k... That's doubling every day. That will be 20k to 40, let's go next to 40 to 80, then 80 to 160 and then from 160 to 320.

Alright there. That's just how you are actually supposed to go and trade it. If you actually work towards... you know as I said "aim for the moon if you lose, you fall down among the stars. This is actually a very very difficult thing to do in real life on a live account anyway but on demo, c'mon risk it all.

So the purpose in this... one way you could use is on a 10k account you can enter as high as 33 lots thereabouts or even much more with a... I think the leverage was as high as 1:500. With 33 lots making about 30pips thereabouts. With 33 lots, a pip will give you $330, times 30 pips giving you 9900 which is approximately 10k. So, let's say... let's add... let's say just 32, we're aiming towards 32 pips. 33 lots. Let me get it accurately now. 10000* divided by 33 = 330. That will be 31 pips there.

Let me take the calculation again in case I happened to have confused you. With 10,000 divided by $330, that will be 30.3 that is why I put it at 31 pips. Unlike now whereby we can actually have a normal pipette. Let's use 31 the highest number possible. So just with 33 lots, you get 31 pips, you can double this 10k account into 20k account. Going for the same number of pips, just a matter of double the lots the next day. That will be 66 the next day and the next day after that will be 132 and keep on doubling every day. You would still go for this same number of pips. Just go for that 31 pips every day consistently, after 5 days, you would be on $320,000.

But now, this very one I won here that I came out 1st, I will show you much latter. This one I won, it was actually a contest that $320,000 couldn't have won because we had to end up the contest with $3million plus.

Okay so, this is one of the record places that LiteForex keeps records of contest winners and so on. They don't actually have a place on their website that that they keep records but they actually do that on several other pages for instance on Money Maker Group and on Talkgold. They actually go out to other forums - money making forums mostly - and then try to talk about contest they are running and "this is how people have performed". But unfortunately, Talkgold and Money maker Group are both websites that are currently down. I think they've been shut down for some practices in the past.

Okay, so if you want to go to these links.... they should be... all these ones should actually be in small cases, small m and son like that. I will actually give you... these links should actually be on the website so you can get to see them there.

So, this is one of the places actually you can be able to find... I had to save it on my system and then... Just go ahead and look for Top10, Forex and Teemy and LiteForex on Google and you will actually find me at this place anyway. When you keep on trading contests after a while, you will see some popular names like this CHRISTALL. I have actually seen him in several other contests I have actually involved myself. This is what I'm talking about Teemy - Top10 contest. Can you see it over here. This is actually $3million here.

So if you had actually raised your account up to what I had recommended here to 320k, you would have been somewhere around this place, you would have been the 5th guy around this guy. You would still have won something though but... in this contest actually I was 1st, I was initially at around 1 million thereabout and I saw this guy actually chasing me and I had to just keep on trading and he too kept on trading or she – I don't know and we kept on trading and at the end of the day I victoriously ended up in this and then I think he too just soloed down there – calmed down after a while. But that was at the last day anyway.

So but the thing is you should be careful because if you're just trying to keep on... to rush higher that the guy above you or the guy below you and you're trying to rush higher, it could actually make you lose the account because remember we are all trading on probabilities. Whereby possibly whether you say yes or no and it is only one of those two that would happen. What if you choose the wrong trade at that time? Is it a buy or a sell what if you placed the wrong trade at that time? Something similarly happened to me last week Friday on a contest I will make sure I show you later on. So, this is just a contest I will never forget because it was really really funny at that period.

This is another example right now... this is a Top10 contest with 520,000. If you take a look at all these, if you have 320,000 you will definitely make... it is actually a guaranteed slot for you to actually get a prize. The prize varies actually but you would definitely get a prize if you are actually around $320,000. Just make sure these are... I think this Vlad is a popular name I see and this is CHRISTALL here again, alright, okay.

So, if you make that $320,000 you would definitely make that 1 million level*. If you make that 320,000 at the end of the 5 days of trading the Top10... LiteForex* Top10 you will definitely make good money in terms of the prizes.

Now, one more thing about the prizes I skipped earlier on, some people will give you prizes... some brokers will give you prizes straight up ahead. As in the full prize, as real cash into your trading account. You can actually straight ahead withdraw that money or you can trade with the money straight up. Some others would give you the money as trading credits. I will explain that again.

I will go back to the beginning again and do that in the summary again . And some actually give you as credits. So that credit you can either use the money to trade and any money you make on your credit is yours but some also give you a limited time that you must trade within so, so and so period like a period of one month otherwise they would nowremove their money. Some also when you trade and you make money and you withdraw any amount, they would actually go ahead and remove their own monies. Actually I will take all that again, I will find a place to slot that in when I'm doing the final editing of the video.

Alright, so let's clean up a little bit and then. That's all with LiteForex Index Master, LiteForex Fighting and LiteForexTop10. At the moment right now, LiteForex is having a contest. Best of the Best. Maybe you guys watched that movie a long time ago? LiteForex is actually having this right now and I've not been able to win it anyway. I easily get kicked out after a while.

Sometimes I have not been having the time to concentrate again on the contest because of busy schedules and I could have placed a trade.... And that's also something you should be careful about when you place a trade and you forget about it or something just takes your time away from it you know. It's possible you can easily can forget about what you've done and when you open your account again you go "Oh ha!" and then...

So, we will talk about how to balance your whole lifestyle and how to balance everything well. Your trading accounts because at the end of the day, you can actually have like 3 or 4 contests you are running at the same time so you should be careful how to make sure you don't go ahead and start losing one and forgetting about the others as well but even at that same time using that kind of trading multiple accounts to actually create a system. I will explain that to you later on.

Alright, let's continue with InstaForex One Million, InstaForex generally.

Chapter 2   -   InstaForex Contests

Alright, let's continue with InstaForex One Million and InstaForex generally. InstaForex One Million is actually a binary options contest.

Let's go to promo. Under promo you'll see various contests. So, this is the One Million contest. Let me open a new tab but this is the registration page and they actually give you how many days to countdown before another new contest starts. You can register for as long as it's not up to one hour to the beginning of the contest. So, this is five days, 19 hours and some minutes. You actually could a have a browser whereby you can use your auto filling functions to drop in all the stuff easily.

Then, so it will... I will auto fill this with my details. I always use Teemy on all my contests but sometimes if I am not able to find Teemy, I would use teemytee or I would use Teemy1, depending on what name they actually allow me to use. Some might actually say they want you to use a number with your name, some want you use like a minimum of six characters and something like that. So this is that. Those are the names I use and then, for this contest, I always try to use sway-free Islamic accounts and then try to fill up the registration. So, that's one way I go about it and this is the homepage of the contest option.

These are currently the contests participants right now. I'm not ranking at all here.

On most of these contests, by the middle of the contest, you should actually be on the first page. This SLONIKS is also another name I see. So, by the middle of the contest, you should actually be on the first page. We have so many pages. Let me scroll a little bit down... there are several pages and then how many traders right here on this contest? 373 traders.

This is a binary options contest, remember. So, by the end of these contest, let me open the archive so you can see few things. By the middle of this contest, remember this is a five day contest, running from Monday to Friday. So by Wednesday, if your name is not on this first page, just don't bother yourself with having a chance at all of ranking anywhere in the first because they only payout the first five for this Million Option contest.

These are the rules for the... the major part... the rules contain the number of places and the winners' amount they will get. It also contains other things like if you are 18 years old and so on like that. One particular thing that is important about this Million Option is, Million Option... let's even go ahead and log in and place a trade.

These are the 11 currencies we can trade on the Million Option. Several things about the InstaForex* contests. The fund prize will be credited to a verified trading account opened by the winner. Prize cannot be withdrawn, however, any profit over the prize amount can be withdrawn without any restrictions. This is what I explained earlier on. These ones, they give you the prize as trading credits so you can trade on that and then, any profit you make is yours but immediately you withdraw any amount, they will withdraw their prize money, they will remove this prize money. So make sure you have enough money…use their amount to make enough profit for yourself before you place any withdrawal and then, of course, the remaining money is yours.

This is the archive, let's go in to see the Participant Cabinet. This is where you would be placing the trades for the Million Option contest on InstaForex*. You don't get to trade on your platform so, there is..; you place trade on the Participant Cabinet. This shows the contests and then the winners. I think... later on but the Million Option... one which was in August 6 2012. So, let's go to 2012.

Now, another thing about the contest is you can actually ahead and see the past contests and see who won amongst the... like, 'yeah, okay, If I get this rating I can also be the first' and so on like that. Just go ahead look at several people win and then... Looking for August 6 here and then you just copy the levels you got to and you can be sure 'Okay alright' actually, when I get there, I can actually make the same position'.

Alright, this is me here. It's even 1380. I think so far so good, this one of the really highest scores I've seen in terms of rating and there's a reason why this Contest Option is really really hard to really pull off in terms of winning. I explained that when we now get to the option trading cabinet. So most of the time, I actually just save the login passwords for the contests on it. It's easy for me to just pull out details without having to look at my sheets. I have my list of contests I've entered and the login details, so I just put in like this.

This is that for this one, I log in and then I would like to take a look at... scrolling down a bit here. This is me and this is my account alright. Everyone starts with a rating of a thousand points from the beginning. So that if you place a trade and you win, you get extra 10 points. If you place a trade AND you lose, you lose 10 points. So far so good, I have lost a net of 7 trades* altogether on this first day of which as it is right now, the gap is just too far away from 1000.

I'm not having the belief that I can actually win this contest but I never can tell until the middle of the contest which is Wednesday before I can give full guaranteed assurance to myself that "okay I can win this or not" but for the purpose of this training, let's just feel free to just use this account.

These are the trades I placed.

Let me just show you an example. If you win, it's green, if you is lose, it's red. So, I made nine losses and two wins. Nine losses minus two wins, that's nine minus two, seven, that's 70 points loss there but what you do is you just have to just predict direction, price is going to either up or down BY a certain point in time. That's one of the reasons why trading binary is actually difficult than trading currencies. It's already difficult enough for you to make money in choosing the direction market would get to. This time choosing a time that prize would get there is actually... is even much harder but it's quite easy in the sense that trading this contest because it's actually a free contest. You don't put out anything, just a matter of just click these four form inputs and then calculate profit and then submit. That's all.

So if I say, EURUSD by this time, 4:40. My time here is 2:34 but 4:40 is actually the same thing a... the broker's platform is actually 2 hours ahead of mine. So, I said by 4:40 which will be 2:40 my own time, we would just have the starting time and I will choose an ending time that by so so and so time, EURUSD must increase. Now, it must not end up in the same price. If it ends up in the same price, I lose that bet but if it increases from the price it was at 4:40 up to the time I said it should exit... the end time, if it does that, then I make money but if it doesn't go up or rather, if stays at the same price or it comes lower, then I lose money. So, I can actually choose the direction of either increase or decrease and I have to be sure that it goes there and then I will make the poin... extra ratings.

Let's just go ahead and do it straight out. So, I click a here, I click Profit and EURUSD would be higher by so so and so. If it's higher – this is my current rating - if it's higher, if I make it, I get this. Otherwise, I get this.

So, I can now click...let's go ahead and buy this. Now, the starting time is very very close the time the page loaded and the ending... you can actually choose any ending time at the period of the day and there's a strategy you can actually use to go ahead and pick out these things. I'll explain some of these ones much later on.

There's also one rule again, you cannot enter this if you are within a space of three minutes to this. Take for instance if you are at 2:... okay let's say... you know there is a two-hour gap already between my local time and the platform here. So, if it's 2:40 here, that is exactly the time here, so there's no way... you can't even be allowed to enter a trade at that same time that the... these are going to start counting.

So, anything you have to do, you have to do it before the next one minute. Within a space of three minutes to this time, I won't be allowed to place a trade and if I place had placed trade before... let me show you.

Let's say I want to repeat another trade on this one I just placed a trade on, I already entered into an option for this currency. 'Please select another pair'. There are still 11 more currencies here... instruments rather here that you can trade.

I will also show an example of the error it would bring when you are within three minutes to that. The time has passed okay.

So, the rules...I've explained the rules but I will actually show you how to go ahead in creating a system whereby you can actually trade these currencies when the time comes.

So, where are we? Let's delete. So, InstaForex One Million just a matter of... is a actually a binary... binary options. Now, online trading actually involves several other markets apart from Binary and Forex. We have Commodities, we have Stocks and Bonds and so on like that but I'm just limited to just Forex and Binary is not really so much of a big thing for me anyway but Forex is my major focus.

Alright, so, that's that about this one and then the rules of any contest when you want to start out. Register, read the rules, look at the past... look at the levels the get to when they are winning and then from there plan out your own strategy how you can go ahead and achieve yours. You can pick another contest here, Promo then scalping.

Sorry, let's start with Sniper rather but we wanted to test out something here. Let me choose GBPUSD or next after GBPUSD or any other one I so desire and let's try placing a trade on it now. Calculate profit, my PC is still slow and then let's say BUY. Look at the time, almost 1 minute to the time. You have to also make sure that it is at least 3 minutes more than the current time. And sometimes, it's also possible that your PC might just... or let me say, you can't just actually place a trade, just refresh the page and you would be able to achieve that.

Sniper contest, this is the contest rules page, this is the registration page, next page and the contest archive and the prize winners. There's a difference between the contest archive and the prize winners. This is the last list in the contest but this one shows those that won the contests.

So, removing those that have been disqualified. So, this is… I'll show you the difference between the two at a latter point.

This is Sniper terms and everything. This is the starting, duration, registration start. The contest runs from Monday to Friday and the prizes from 1st to 5th there. It's a contest that starts with $10,000, leverage is 1:500 by default, minimal trading volume is 0.1 lot, maximum is 1 lot and the maximum number of open trades at once even including pending orders is 5. Stop out level is 10 percent. I don't think anybody has ever achieved this because… I will show you examples right now.

This is an example of… this is… you can see the contest here has a balance of $10,000. So, definitely out of these actually this one is the Sniper contest. Alright, I've been in this trade already since yesterday morning. This is the contest I entered 4 trades on GBOUSD and 1 trade on GBPJPY. So, this is… let me close these ones and show you exactly. I entered 1 lot here, why would I enter the minimum of 0.1 when I can actually enter a lot size much higher than that. That's the highest I can even go anyway. So, I have to accept this to do fast closures and opening of trades. So, lets say New Order… so, to make it fast, you can use pressing with one hand F9 and the other hand pressing the mouse*. I am just trying to replace back what I deleted.

Alright, so, we have over here one particular set of rules there that 5% of your profit must be derived from GBPUSD and 5% of your profits must be derived from GBPJPY. Any amount can be derived from both of them anyway but the thing is that, at least 5% must come from GBPUSD and at least 5% from GBPJPY. That's all.

Now in this contest, you really need to… it's a contest that you actually have to achieve a whole lot of pips for you to win and for you to do that, I would recommend you using currency like GBPCAD, GBPNZD and GBPAUD because these guys actually move a lot. They're actually fast… the currencies that have large movements. I think I have a tool here that analyses currencies. No particular input features. So, over here, what it does is to analyze currencies, the spread, the daily average movement. Let me try and restart this guy…

Alright, we have GDPAUD, GBPNZD, GBPJPY also has a large daily average. Where is GBPCAD, where are you? Okay, you just need to refresh… So, then, all of them here, we are able to see their daily average movements and you can see which currencies will pay you more in terms of movement though the spreads of these ones are actually high anyway. These ratios are just a matter of getting the mathematical division of daily average by the spread just to give you thins, there is no big deal about this but the currencies that actually will give you good movements are GBPAUD and GBPNZD.

So, I have to just move back and forth to refresh this to get the full list (Indicator updated). GBPCAD, that's 133 pips, GBPAUD and GBPNZD. I will explain little about these things together while trying to explain… give you a view how you can trade Million Option later on. There is something called correlation. It actually works with these currencies. I'll explain that one later.

That is the total of building a trading system at another time. This time, I will be talking about just going ahead to just win the contests. Anytime it comes to trading systems then I will explain all that. Though this is not a video book for trading systems but I will just branch into it a bit and give you just a little better view of how to balance your instruments.

Alright, we're talking about Sniper contest. Now, InstaForex* has other contests too that are like Sniper, so, I might as well just mention them right now. So, from promo… contest…now some of them are actually Lottery contests but this one is actually real trading contest like Chancy Deposit you can really know that that's one of such Lottery contests.

Now there is this contest, Real Scalping* is similar to Sniper, which I just explained just now which you must make 5% from GBPUSD and 5% from GBPJPY. Also Real Scalping is also the same thing as Sniper only that with Sniper, the whole trading happens within a period of 1 week. Real Scalping runs for like a month. From the first Monday of the month to the last Friday of the month and then Rally FX is a 1-day contest which is on Friday only. Similarly, you must also make 5% of your account GPPUSD and another 5% at least minimum from GPPJPY.

These three are similar and in InstaForex Sniper, you need to make 2500…you start with 10,000. You need to make extra 2500…so, that's 12,500 for you to be a contest winner and this is with the contest archive. That should give you a glance of how much you must make to achieve that.

For the other one which is not here, that is InstaForex Real Scalping, you need to raise it from… You start from 20,000 to 5000 more, that's $25,000 at the end of a 1-month program. So, this is InstaForex Sniper archive. You can actually search for names of traders or your own name using this search options. PC is still slow but at least it should carry us through before I go back to sleep.

While that's still loading. Reasl Scalping, you raise it from $20-$25,000. So, it's like… what we're just doing is you're just making extra 2500 twice in a period of… when you have a period of a full one month - four weeks to go but it's like what you made in Sniper within one week. Just do it twice and then you are actually a winner on this. So, if you achieve this in a week, you can actually trade two weeks out of the whole four weeks and you're actually a winner getting this.

The other one…the third one which I mentioned is the Rally FX1. That one, you start with an account of 40,000. You have to make around 15,000 extra. So, that'll be 55,000 there. The maximum you can trade on this one is 1 lot and a maximum of 5 trades altogether both pending and open orders. Similarly, this one, 5 trades maximum, 1 lot is the maximum but over here, it's 10 lots and you can place 7 trades maximum. 10 lets, you enter a trade for 10 lots –each one and you can run 7 trades on it. 7 trades-10 lots, 5 trades-1 lot , 5 trades-1 lot each on this one. But Great race is similar to all of them also but it's a little bit different in the sense that it starts with a 100,000 and you try as much as possible to raise to 40,000 extra. That'll be 140,000 and then you are a winner but in it's own case, there's n…let me just do this.

Let me start with Sniper. So, 1 lot 5 trades and 5% GBPUSD, 5% GBPJPY. There you go. Same thing here but this one, 10 lots maximum and 7 trades but on this one, 10 lots maximum, 5 trades and there is no limitation on this one on this one. They actually run InstaForex Great Race for four times in a year… five actually but the first four times are like qualifiers for the final one. So, let's check out Great Race.

Let's go on to what I wanted to show you before which is this. So, this is the Sniper which I told you that you should just go ahead and make that 2500 on top of your 10,000 to win the contest. This guy only made 1,610 and he is number one.

So, let's verify another period in the list. Let's just jump to any one. We already jumped to another date, so, you'll have… the whole thing will refresh and give us another period and sets of people and sets of winning goals. So, if you use that to evaluate and see what you actually should be winning to achieve... This 1900, they did not even make it up to 2000 anymore. I know it's difficult anyway. It's not as it it's that easy but the thing is, just work towards as I said aim for the moon if you fall you'll land among the stars, that kind of thing. If you aim for the stars, you'll land among the trees... whatever.

So, okay...let me show you one last... one final one. This is 1,900. Anyway, go for this. And try to achieve... what you would work towards achieving this. So, I want to go and do the problem of Real Scalping for you. You can do that on your own and InstaForex Rally, this is in it also. You can work at these ones on a normal day not about when something like a Brexit news comes out and everything just 'phew'... scatters the whole market. I am talking about these are normal days. Actually, let me just show you this one.

Alpari Virtual Reality is a contest that runs for two and half months. When the - is it Fracageddon or whatever it is that it is being termed now, the news on the swi... this unfortunate incident that happened about the Swiss Franc when the Cap was removed just for a few moments on that day 15 – 1 – 15, year 2015 January 15th. Someone actually happened to have placed only just...I think...yeah, just three trades, he caught the upward movement, he caught the downward movement and he had already had placed one trade before then and that was all. He didn't place any trade again throughout the whole period and he came first.

So, sometimes, some of those fantastic news, they just changed the whole playing field but the thing is this; everybody had the same opportunity, so, if someone was chanced enough to just utilise his own either by luck or just be coincidentally is... at that period, it's his bonus.

This one would be opening up in the next... it'll be starting in the next 26 days. Let's go to the rules which is what I want to show you. It's starting in the next 26 days and this are the number of people that already registered with a starting account balance of $100,000, I'll go to the contest archive to view the past winners.

I want to show you something else also. Okay, let me just type it straight up. That'll be Million Option... Million archive. Now, this is what I want to show you about the rules. I told you about Great Race earlier before. I said it runs four times in a year but actually five times in the sense that the first four times are actually qualifiers for the last round. So these are the dates for the year, these are the dates for the normal... these are the dates... from this number 1 to 11, these are the prizes, these are for the first four rounds and then, the final is actually the prizes are actually much more higher than that of the first four rounds.

So, everybody... even if you don't win anything, you can actually still enter here but the people over here, these last guys, they have gotten bonus points. So, if a person is with a bonus point of 40 bonus points, he's actually going to get extra 40,000. Every point is $1,000. So, if you have 40 bonus points, you're going to have $40,000. That is plus a $100,000, you're going to have $140,000 even before the contest starts and you still have to beat that, so, how do you do that?

So, this is Forex Option archive. I wanted to show you something and that was in January of what year was that again? All right, I was going to show you this is this. January 18th of 2016. This is the Million Option contest archive. I was first here, anyway and this FEARGREED was on number 4. By the end of the contest, they did the whole thing, FEARGREED came out as number one. He was formerly number 4 if you can remember. So meaning 1, 2 and 3 were disqualified for various reasons. I was disqualified because I was told that I used...I logged in with… I opened two contest accounts of which I didn't actually but it's quite easy to fall into that kind of mistake because I was using a modem to browse and if you're using a modem and you have an IP and someone else, coincidentally entering the same contest also is assigned that IP within that period of that one week the contest was running, of course the broker's server will just record it as 'this person having two accounts'.

So, you'll try to avoid a modem. Actually, in the rules, they actually advise against using modems to browse… for the contest anyway – let me out it that way - just to avoid that kind of clash. In mostly… all brokers, actually, tell you not to open multiple accounts because it's against… it increases your chances of winning and it's against the rules but if you are trading on live contests, I don't think anyone is going to discourage you from having multiple accounts on live contests mostly. So, you are always like having… it happens mostly on demo accounts. They tell you open only just one contest account and unfortunately, if something like a modem could work against you… it's not something that happens every time. It is not as if everybody in your country is using the same network and all of them are all trading contests from the same broker and entering, you know… It's not as if that kind of chance would happen regularly. It's something that happens just once in a while and of course, it was just that one time it happened.

So, yes, similarly some people have been moved away because of me in the past and not intentionally because of me, anyway but I too was moved away for FEARGREED at another time. So, it can happen to anybody. Whatever it is, whatever the rules you fall under – in the rules it is part of their terms you have to follow by any rules and any decision and their decision is final. You really can't say anything about it.

So, yes, it can happen. Anybody can be disqualified but to avoid being disqualified, avoid using things like general public or a modem that has a general IP address that is dynamic and can be assigned at any time to anybody. That's one of the ways you can avoid being disqualified.

Chapter 3 - More Contests

3,1 (Alpari Virtual Reality)

Alright, let's go back to Alpari which is the last one on the list here which we haven't talked about. Alpari Virtual Reality... usually, Alpari has several contests, both demo and live. This is Alpari's own binary options, Trader Wars like pitching traders against one another and still entering the contest. It's actually a live contest. You actually enter I think with $50 or so. If you want to really know about it, just go through here and then, on the page, on the very page, you'll see somewhere below, the contest rules. So you will read everything about the contest.

This is the Virtual Reality contest, if you click on it, you will come back to this page here. This is the Virtual Reality contest. It runs for about two and a half weeks, it runs every quarter. So this is... it's actually 11 weeks to be exact. This one started from the 16th of April, it will be ending on the 30th of June. Today is the 27th, which means there's just a few days to go. So, by now, everybody here knows where they are. It is only those that are trying to get into this ranking spot that that will keep on trying and these guys are in the ranking spots from number 1 to number 20. These are the guys going home with something.

Remember I told you, a hundred Alpari points is $1.00. So, this guy actually has $100 to collect if he's able to retain this spot or she.

This is the ranking. Alpari ranking is not just a matter of just getting to the highest position because this guy made the highest in profits. This is the ranking based on that but this guy is number two based on something else. There is another set of parameters being used, which is the drawdown and the profit factor and I'll explain both of them right now. The drawn down is like... is the amount of... is like how far negative your account went percentage-wise when you were trading.

To really make a good... actually, everybody will have drawdown at the end of the day but maybe to an extent it's actually variable, one to another but the thing is if you use lower lot sizes, you will have lesser drawdowns anyway of course, meaning you will have lesser profits but the main thing at the end of the day, you'll discover that if you actually focus more on this and are constantly making pips, you will actually end up being on the top ranking here. Let me show you an example here.

This is Alpari Virtual Reality results. The results page is somewhere... normally it is supposed to be somewhere close around here before but I don't know why.... I would actually have to look for it. This is the result of winners in the past but you have to actually look for the results. In this case now, I found the result round number 32... 35 here which was last year... the third quarter of last year. I came out 26th. I actually... take a look here and see I am number 40, I have the highest ranking in terms of the account balance. In the real sense, in two and a half months, you should be able to do something in terms of achieving this even if you're using your lower lots* but unfortunately, my draw down was just too high and my Profit Factor was just too low. The Profit Factor is the ratio of the profits you've made over the losses you have accrued. So, it's an inverse of your drawdown in a way. If you have a high draw down, your Profit Factor will definitely be lower. The main focus is to actually have a lower drawdown. If you can get your drawdown to be very very low, yeah, you can easily get a high Profit Factor. Low drawdown, consistent pips, you are good to go.

There's this contest here... the round 29 which was January two years ago, January 2018 but unfortunately, I can't find data here. Over here, I was even the first. My account was I think, 400% plus thereabout but unfortunately with losing out of the drawdown and the Profit Factor. I was actually good for a month and half. I was actually ranking well, I was like first 7 or so. All of a sudden, my drawdown was just getting too much and then, everything just went the other way. So, that was how I got to drop out of the contest but unfortunately, I don't have the data. I would have actually shown you that.

So, it is really good to see yourself ranking well somehow but unfortunately, when other factors are bringing you down, you don't feel so good with yourself.

The thing is, make sure you constantly make good profits but with lesser drawdown. How do you do this? Alpari has a leverage of 1:10 which is in itself is a means of encouraging you to use lower lot sizes. It reduces your chance of just using high leverages. This other account actually has 1:500 similar to almost every other thing here as well but Alpari is telling you "use this low leverage*".

When contests are organized, your brokers actually give you a glimpse of what they expect you to do even when you're trading with them in real life. For instance, Exness has a contest giving you a leverage of 1:2000*... I can't say exactly. I think I should o back to cross-check that... so, meaning that this is a broker that actually encourages you to use high lots when trading with them live. They are actually showing themselves in terms of "This is what we expect of you when you come around to trade with us live.". Remember I told you contest is a way of getting promotions, getting you to come around to their brokerage to see them in action and then if you really like their performance so far, then, you feel like okay you can open an account and then do that. They have encouraged you to really trade as much as you can. That's Exness for you and so, Alpari is telling you that,"based on this contest we expecting you to make consistent profits gently." 'Gently' meaning with lower lot sized, not risking too much of your account. So, if you have a low draw down and consistent you will be good. You'll actually have a balanced account at the end of the day.

Let me just give a little evaluation of those that are in the current contest. This one. Let's see. This guy is in number 1 here having this. His draw down is 6% and his profit factor is this. So, he has... let me see who has the lowest drawdown. This is what you actually use when you're working now. You are having a low drawdown of 3%. Let's check over here as well. The guy having rank of 50 is having a drawdown of 3% and so on like that. Let's assume for you to do very well here, you should have a drawdown of nothing more than 2.5%. Let's say 2.5%, a very low drawdown of 2.5%. How many pips do you think you actually need to achieve you know, number 1 here? We'll do the calculation and work out the same way we did all these ones as well. We'll be doing all of them all together. Alright, so what else? I think I've done that part.

We will now go to the mathematical part of getting how many pips you would need to achieve all of these targets. Mathematics now, you'll start with that of Alpari. Alpari is a contest you start with 100,000 and then, from what you could see here, those ranking highest.... the person ranking highest right now is getting it at... he is on 100% profit.

So, let's say you want to aim towards 200% profits within the duration of the contest every Forex trading month is 22 trading days or let's use 20 - the lower of the two - 20 days in a month and the contest is two and half months. So altogether, we'll be talking about 50days of contest trading and you want to make 200% profit during that duration and you want to risk nothing more than... as we said, everybody here is... the person who has the lowest draw down and yet is still ranking here is 3.-something percent. So, let's say 2.5%. You don't want draw anything lower than 2.5 percent drawdown limit.

How do you achieve this? About 50 trading days. Let's say you're going to be trading every single day. If you are trading every single day, in 50trading days, you want to achieve 200%*. You're going to have the 200 divided by 50, in the calculator, that's 4% daily. You want to achieve a profit of 4% on your account daily. You're going to be trading every day. Just 4% every day and then don't go less than 2.5%.

I don't know how the trading system you have at the moment is effective but the thing is, if you enter trades based on just let's say risking 1.5%, let's say you enter risking about 1.5 percent per trade, do that three times and you have a win-loss ratio of winning 2 and losing 1. At the end of the day, you're left with 4.5. ***

Let's talk about having 3 trades. You are risking... (I'm going to cut this off). Let's change this to 3 just for easier calculation. I'll explain why. So, you don't want to lose more than 3% of your account and you want to achieve 4% of your account every single day so, this is how you go about it. You will risk 1% per trade and the purpose of the trade is to make sure that you don't... you do something like say, risking 20 pips to achieve 40 pips No, it couldn't be 40. Let's get the exact calculation we're talking about here. This is the calculator I will be giving you as a bonus. Now Alpari starts with a balance of 100,000 which is to make * 4% rather. Let's say we want you to risk 1, let's try 1.5 and the other one being 2. Our Stop Loss, what's going to be our Stop Loss when we start? Let's say we want to put as our Stop Loss, let's say 20 pips Stop Loss in* our trades. At this level and a Standard Lot is 100,000 anyway. At this level, if you want to risk just one percent, the lot size you will be using is 4.35 lots* per trade, our StopLoss is 20 pips and we have to go to achieve 92 pips every single day or you could say you could place the same trade four different times or making 92 divided by 4. I think I need a calculator now. Alright 92 divided by 4, that's 23 actually. Okay, 96 is 24. So, 23 pips on each go. You are going to be getting four trades on each go but if you really are someone that just enter a trade risking 23 pips hoping to make double that or hoping to make 2%, so you're going for 46 pips every trade risking 20 pips having a 20 pip Stop Loss.

Now if you are good enough actually, two trades in just one day, you'll get to that your 4% if you want to achieve but if you are not so lucky, you might win two and let's say lose one. So, win two, that'll be 46 times 2, that'll be 92 and if you lose one that'll be minus 23 considering the spread depending on what... I really need to put that of Alpari's accrued spread there but depending on the currency you're trading on which anyway and also, Alpari uses a variable spread but the spread is actually low, anyway . So, that will be like, if you lose, you lose like 23, if you win, you win 46 which is actually a good win-loss ratio, anyway, 1:2.

So, you just make sure you make a net profit of two trades overall, a net profit of two trades every single day. So, if you're one of those that actually enter four trades, if you win two, if you lose one, you are still off the mark but if you win let's say three and then you lose one, then you are really really good on the mark.

So, it's not a matter of catching too many pips actually because we talk about pip effectiveness. So, it's either you enter four trades overall making 92 pips or you enter just two trades at each of them going for… okay, four trades going for 23 pips or two trades for 46 pips or just one trade going for pips altogether. The main target every single day is just to make that 92 pips out of all the whole 28 currency pairs you are allowed to trade. Just make out 96 pips out every day and while doing that, 92 pips per day will give you your 4%. ***

So, at 92 pips a day, risking… so if you are risking 1%, you have to get 92 pips overall or depending on if you want to get 92 pips at once, you can get that, then you're good or you can get it at 46 pips making it twice or try it four times just making 23 pips at each go. I know I probably ended up confusing you a little but it's a video you can go back again and watch over it again but another thing I don't want to go over it again is I want you yourself take the calculator and do the mathematics yourself. So, more like an assignment for you to do.

Alright, so you just make sure you just go for every single day, 92 pips and then you are good to go. You are on your way to making this amount and remember you're just risking 1% at each time you're placing a trade. That way, that reduces your chances of having a high drawdown.

And also, one more thing. Alpari closes your trade at the close of market every day. Alpari closes any running trade and re-opens it. So, in case you happen to be in a negative on that trade, you're going to have a… it's going to close at a negative against you and another new trade opens and that trade that closed as a negative comes back as part of your drawdown.

So, you might actually feel, "Oh, I can leave a trade to run for a long time as long as even if it's running negative, it's going to come back as positive and I'm going to close it back when it is positive." No, Alpari doesn't give you that chance. They actually close all your trades whether positive or negative at the close of market day, every single day and reopens. The same lot, the same TakeProft and StopLoss, the same levels there but the thing is the trade closes. Meaning that if you are in negative, you're going to have your draw down. So, that's a way to ensure that everybody has a drawdown even if they… and so, nobody can cheat because of that even if they are running a long term trade. So, ensure your trades are always in positive as at that time or you altogether avoid trading towards the end of close of market day so as to ensure that you don't have an negative drawdown if you are not sure which direction the market would first go on a trade you are in. I think that should cover that.

Let's be sincere with ourselves. You probably don't have a chance to trade all 50 trading days, so in short, let me just put it this way. Get as many pips as you can every single day but know that this is your threshold minimum and in getting this but of course, I said shoot for the sky, you fall among the trees I think so that way, you at least get a good value that you will be achieving a high profit ranking for your balance. That's just like this one over here, this is 100%/ The thing is you can actually really do this in demo making 20% in a period of two and half months, 200% extra. If you are really a good trader but then, this is another extra money you can be making extra on it and Alpari prizes are all withdrawable but I think with a clause. I didn't really win any particular contest. I didn't really win anything much per se during my own except for this one that I made 1000 Alpari points.

3,2 (Extra Contests)

Let's go back to InstaForex contests. InstaForex Real Scalping, I mean I never won that but I will explain that because it is actually similar to the Sniper which I won. So this is a Sniper, you only need to just make this amount within a period of one week. Let me add duration: 1 week. Don't worry, I will give you this workbook. Real Scalping is 4 weeks, it starts from the first Monday of the month, ends on the last Friday of the month.

Rally, it's just on Fridays and Great Race is one month. Good, so let me explain all of this. I told you if you are able to achieve keep these extras on the top of them, you can actually get to a prize winning position. Okay, so we have Sniper. In Sniper you just need to make $250. I think I left one contest running here. All right so, here we… alright here, this one yes. So, it is exactly a Sniper contest so… there we go. Don't let it bug you if you lose any contest. Remember it's not real… It's just a bonus money anyway so don't try to make… let it pain you if you lose. Anyway, someone is supposed to lose and someone is supposed to win.

Here I am running negative here. I'm actually running 5 trades. See what I said here, 5 trades here but with the… make sure that on GBPUSD and GBPJPY, you must make 5% extra. And also, you can't be trading the same way you would be trading on demo the same way you trade your live accounts, hope you know that because as you've noticed here, there's no Stop Loss. I don't trade without Stop Loss and I don't use high lot sizes. Well, let me say I'm not supposed to use high lot sizes because that had been one of the things that has affected me in the past*. Using too much could help you end your account and as well if it's part of you, you end up losing your contest accounts also. So well the thing is, if you really want to make it on these ones, you definitely won't have time to put Stop Loss because of a lot of things. You are probably trading your live account at the same time amongst other things and try to avoid making mistakes. I've actually heard of an instance where someone was trading and someone came to his laptop and placed a trade and he went into a loss and he was like "wow I didn't know it was a… I thought it was a demo account" but it was a live account and the person lost money. Alright, so be careful about that that's on a normal live… don't make that kind of mistake by yourself and enter a contest… on your live account what you normally would have entered on a contest account and don't let it spoil your trading habits, okay. Try to differentiate between the two of them. One is for fun and one is real.

Alright so, one thing about the InstaForex contest is it has a different server on its own, this server: InstaForex-1Contest.com. Before it used to be just this: InstaForex-Contest.com. Now InstaForex has a Multiterminal, so what I used to do then was that I would have most of those contests that I'm entering into that are on InstaForex that I can enter on the platform, I would enter all of them on the Multiterminal at once. But immediately they changed the server to this InstaForex-1Contest.com and the server was* not on the Multiterminal, I couldn't get to enter it. This Multiterminal is not like this normal trading terminal whereby you can change the contest server and put your own server there but on the Multiterminal, the servers are fixed and you can't change it from what's there already.

Update: InstaForex has now included 1Contest server on their Multiterminal*.

That's just by the way. Let's come back, we are trying to calculate that for Sniper what you need to do every single day. Maximum you can enter 5 trades as I am showing you right now in this example. So, 5 trades and 5% must be from GBPUSD and 5% from GBPJPY minimum*. Altogether I made it $2500. Alright, let's say you are entering a trade at once, all of them, that means all together, you are trading 5 lots altogether at once because there is no point in trading 0.01 lot and also if you look at the margin level. I said that you really can't go wrong at all. You really can't even wipe out this account even if you wanted to. Alright, so in this limit now you have the entirety of 5 trades. So altogether this is 2500 in 5 trading days, 1 week. So, let's start. Let's put this one lower, let's clean out this guy. For Sniper, I will explain right now. So, we have $2500 in 5 trading days divided by 5 that's $500 per day. That's the profit you are going for. Since you have five trades, you can enter five trades at the same time so it will now 500 divided by 5.

Yeah one more thing, just as I showed you in this calculator here, over here, InstaForex accounts standard lots are 10,000 units not the normal standard 100,000 units you see on most brokerages. So, this means that 1 lot would give a profit of $1 unlike the other 1 lot giving $10 account types right. So $500 per day divided by 5 lots, you need to achieve 100 pips. You need to achieve 100 pips to do that. It's just that simple. You just have to find a good trading system to give you 100 pips a day.

Actually in most of the contests if you go for 100 pips every day, you actually should be a winner. In all the contests if you can achieve100 pips a day you are actually a winner. If you can do that on a real life account provided your Stop Loss is also something low something like in the other scenario we said if your Stop Loss is like 20 pips and achieving this you are making 4%. So if you are actually going for this every single day you should be able to win the Sniper contest.

For the Real Scalping I will just quickly explain that. You just need to make 2,500 sorry… you need to make 5000 above the 20,000 here which is just double what you did here. If you actually do this in two weeks. Do this in week 1, week 2 and for the remaining two weeks go on a break. Meaning it is quite easier to win this Real Scalping compared to even Sniper but you can actually do this cal calculation separately. That is 5000 divided by – how many trading days in this scenario which is it would actually be double of the 50 pips - let's go on divided by how many trading days? 4 weeks, 20 trading days, divided by 20 that will be 250. No no no no no. what is wrong with me? 5000 divided by 20, 250 that is 250 per day. Good. So that will be $250 per day, let me put this there. So, $250 per day divided by 5 equals to 50. 50 pips a day. Just go ahead and get your 50 pips every single day. If you're going to be trading the whole 20 trading days or just replicate what you can on Sniper, get 100 pips every day for the first 2 weeks and you can go on a break for the remaining 2 weeks. Other contestants won't be going on break anyway. So it is better you see it through to the end. The thing is just go for this every single day and you would be able to make the extra 5000 on top of the 20000 and then you are good to go.

Alright so we move on to the Rally and Great Race. Before we do that, let's calculate our 5% on GBPUSD and GBPJPY. For this one, if you are going to make 500 pips here, that means a minimum of just 5 pips net profits, 5 pips for GBPUSD and remember that Yen has a dollar value that's lesser than that of the dollar. That would be around 7 pips for GBPJPY. I am not going to calculate this because if you've been a good trader because a good trader can win this Oh God!

Okay Alright, let me go ahead and get this out for you.

We know $1 is $1, what is $1 in Yen? Say $1 in USD equals to at the moment 110.43 Yen. So how many Yens would we need to be able to achieve it's own 5%? In it's own case. 1 pip = $1 so that will be 1 divided by 110.43 that is 0.009 and since the yen is 2 decimal placed lesser than other pairs. Multiplied by 100, it's actually 0.9*. That will be 1 divided by 110.45 equals to this then multiplied by 100, that will be 0.9. If you want to achieve 5%, that will be 5 divided by 0.9, divided by 0.903 to be exact, that's 5.5 that's 6 pips. This will be a net profit of 6 pips for GBPJPY every single day to get its own 5% per day.

So, make this amount in pips for GBPUSD and this for GBPJPY every single day or should we say for the period of a whole one week this one times 5, that will be 25 pips per week net profit of that for that week and for GBPJPY, net profit of… for GBPJPY that would be 6 times 5, that will be 30 pips per week for GBPJPY. So to get it's own 5% throughout the whole period. So altogether, this is what we are looking for. If you are going to achieve $2500 in 5 trading days, that will be $500 per day. $500 per day is actually 100 pips if you are going to run all 5 of your permissible trades at once but you must make sure you get this amount 5 pips for GBPUSD, 6 pips for GBPJPY every single day or this amount in this and this that is if you are also running all 5 trades at once for these ones.

Now for a similar scenario for Real Scalping, remember this one is for Sniper. In a similar scenario for Real Scalping, you need to for the 5%, so 5% of this is 2.5 pips for GBPUSD or for GBPJPY that will be 2.5… that will be 5, 6, 3.0. 3.0 pips for GBPJPY per day. So if you are going to make this for the duration of 20 days. That will be 20 times this. That will be 50 pips for GBPUSD for the whole duration of the 4 weeks and for GBPJPY, you need to make 3.5 times 20 that's 70 pips, net profit pips for GBPJPY. But of course you can't get 2.5 pips, no this is 3.0 thank you very much. This is 2.5 pips, you can't get 2.5 pips anyway so let's sat that's about 3 pips everyday. So if you can just go ahead and get this and get this any time during the duration you can actually more like you've freed yourself from the problem of having to watch out for GBPUSD and GBPJPY trade setups.

Alright we can move this guy here, move ok. So we should have enough space for...

For the Rally, I told you the Rally is quite similar to the Sniper only that it's a 1 day contest, it takes place on just one day during the… during every week. The profit here is supposed to be 15,000 and it's a 1 day contest. I said you can trade up to 10 lots at once and have a maximum of 7 trades altogether so we have each trade can actually give you 70 pips not 700 – 70 pips. So it is just a matter of launching all 7, running all 7 like that and each of them having 10 10 lots. A pip movement would give you $70. So 15,000* divided by 70. So you have to catch a total of 214 pips. 215 to be exact to really be accurate there. You need to catch 215 pips every single day for this particular contest.

It is not always all the time that kind of thing happens that people go ahead and get this large amount but it's actually possible that people do get this large amount. There is a reason why. I will go to that later on as we talk other contests. And then for the GBPUSD and GBPJPY, 5% of that is how many pips you should get on that is… assuming you are running either GBPUSD on all seven slots and GBPJPY on all seven slots, that will be just, 5% of this is 215 multiplied by 5 then divided by 100. So, that's 10.75 that will be for GBPUSD, that will be 10.75 well lets say 11 pips, 11 net profit for GBPUSD and for GBPJPY that will be approximately that will be like 12, maximum 13 let's say… let's just say 13 pips, I don't want to do any calculation right now 13 pips for GBPJPY. Alright, let us do the calculation. That will be 11 pips. I said a pip is actually 1 divided by sorry... 1 divided by 110.45 or so earlier on multiplied by 100 because of the extra 2 decimal places. That's 0.905, multiply that by 11. 11 divided by 0.905 sorry, that will be 11 divided by 0.905 gives you 12. ... that's 13 yeah. 13 pips for GBPJPY the net profit for you to get that for the duration of just one day.

So make sure if you run all seven trades on GBPUSD and you get this or all seven trades on GBPJPY you must net this for that.

So the next thing we would be talking about is the Great Race Contest which is making $40,000. 40,000 over a duration of 20 trading days of one month. Let me leave space here. 20 trading days of one month that is $2000 per day. So if you want to make your $2000 per day and you can use 5 trades at once and 10* lots for each trade, that will be you will be entering 50 lots at once. So divided by 50 as a set which is equal to 40 pips. Luckily in this case... in this scenario... in this case, we don't have any extra limitations as to make sure we have 5% on GBPUSD and 5% on GBPJPY.

Just go on ahead and just make 40 pips every single day and after 20 trading days you would be on 40,000 but if it so happens that you are entering the contest on the last round and you are just entering for the first time, and then of course the last round which is the 5th round, remember the first four rounds, everybody is on open field but the last round, some of the people that actually have won contest prizes in the first four rounds, some of them get thousands of dollars*. The highest so far gets extra 40,000 dollars* more. That means the person starts with 140,000 while you are just starting with 100,000. So if you are really going to beat this guy who has 140,000, that means you are going to be going for double that. You are going to make 80,000 so as to at least beat the guy that an extra chance over you. So in this case, instead of 40 pips, you'll be going for 80 pips in that scenario. If you are going to go for 80,000, you have to just double that go for 80 pips a day so as to match up with the guy that has been leading you. Now let me explain this.

Let me go to... let's open InstaForex*. This is a Great Race contest that ended April. Let me use this 2016 example of Great Race 1,2,3,4,5 so this one is the contest that ended let's say 5th final round. This is one of the first round contests ending in 144,000. Can you see the first is over 40,000 anyway. This is the second here, it is only the first few guys that will be I think, yeah, first 11, we've seen that earlier before that actually get prizes. So now let's check out on the 5th round in one of the years I just brought out to see ... This is a Great Race contest that has a deposit price of around 180,000. This is the contest itself, Great Race 2015. Compare that to one of the previous four contests... previous four rounds for that same year. The prize of the first guy should be around... this is different. So we even have some that could actually achieve this on a normal day. So just take note. That means let's up our target then. 80 pips every day. 80 pips everyday for the Great Race contest.

For the Great Race contest, the prizes are from the 1st to the 11th, we will have this and on the fifth round the prizes almost like doubled. That that win in the first round that are on this lover level from the 7th to the 11th will have these points. Someone that has these 40 bonus points would be given additional 40,000 that is 1000 per point, he would be given 40,000 at the beginning* of the next contest he registers for. Immediately he registers for the contest, he sends InstaForex tournament department an email and they now deposit the bonus into his account... into his demo account. This one would normally have been paid into his live account and this one will be paid into the new 5th round demo account and he can now trade with that and actually he already has an edge over every other person. Even though you are from here to here number 7th to number 11 in the first four rounds at any point, you are not to worry, you can actually add it all together and achieve something here in the fifth round and of course, the prizes are much more and that would be all for InstaForex contests. Except one more.

Chapter 4 - Doing the Math

Now there is another InstaForex contest. This is something I will give out to you as an extended service for those that actually bought this book. More and more of it will be coming with further contest so let me just give you this even though I myself I haven't won this yet, InstaForex... but I almost did last week. Well possibly would have and that is the Lucky Trader. Guess I wasn't lucky with that contest.

This is a contest that you start with an amount of 30,000, this is exactly the same contest I am entering over here. You enter a maximum of 10 trades... you enter from 10 trades. It's own target is 5000 extra that will be 35,000* but is not as straightforward as that and I will explain it now. In its own case you have 1 lot and 10 trades, 10 pips each and that is quite different. This is how it goes. For Lucky trader, if you win 1 pip, you win 1 point. So if you make 10 pips, you make 10 points but if you make 100 pips, you still make 10 points because the maximum you can actually achieve at any step is 10 points*. So even if you make 10 pips or a million pips, it's still 10 points once you close it. So for you to really maximize the full distance of that 100 pips, you need to actually go ahead and make the 10 pips 10 times to make 10 points, 10 points at each step. Actually, you won't actually net 10 times in 100 pips because the spread is actually going to be included in between so let's say a maximum of like say 7 or 8 times. So that's the way to actually effectively use your pips.

So that is why this EA I have here is going to actually close the trade at just exactly 10 pips. So once it is 10 pips it closes the trade for me in profit. This is actually a scalping... I call this EA Scaping Multiterminal in the sense that... where are you? There. It is just like more like for a purpose of scalping. I don't actually trade scalping in real life anyway but this is a contest and follow the rules. It determines the way you trade it.

Alright, so it is actually meant to just catch 10 pips. If it catches 10 pips, it opens another 10 trades again and keeps on going that way. Take for instance I was on EURUSD and I had placed a sell instead, these are all buy trades. If I had used the EA to place a sell trade so that it would be catching 10 pips all the way since it is at 80, we would be probably about had like 6 runs all together thereabouts now and that is if I was on the right anyway but the main thin... and unfortunately, if I lose... like if I close right now if I lose... if I closed the trade right now and lost, I would be losing this whole 41 pips compared to if I was having... and this would have been 41 points against me compared to if let's say I made 41 pips profits but I would only be recorded with only 10 points. So the full brunt of losing would be against me if I lose but if I win, maximum I can only be given is 10 pips. So take note. For you to actually win this contest, this is how it goes.

We want to make the sum of 5000 throughout the whole contest, the contest runs for 2 weeks, 2 weeks which is 10 trading days. So divided by 10. In the real sense, we are actually looking towards points here not even pips actually. So 5000 points. So we want to make... so divided by 10 trading days which is 2 weeks, that will be 500 pips... that is 500 points per day and to make 5000 points, remember that we can enter a total of 10 trades at once that's for 10 lots, so that's divided by 10 equals to 50. What we want to do is we want to achieve making 50 pips every single day, we want to net 50 pips in that... that will be 5 different times, 10 pips - 5 different times altogether to achieve this. Just go for everyday place one trade 10... as in one trade 10 pips, another trade 10 pips, do it 5 times in a day and you are good to go. So you would have made... you would have made 50 pips on each day or altogether 500 pips altogether for each day and doing it for the whole 10 days of the contest, you will be stopping it at this... at 5000 there.

So it's just a matter of just going for 50pips every day, 50 net pips every day but you would have to be stopping it at 10 pips every single time you are entering a trade. To make this easier for me, I use this Scalping Multiterminal.

What else? Next.

For whatsoever reason on EURJPY I want to place a trade. Allow live trading I will enter a buy trade and okay then allow this. So it will enter all the buy trades. 10 buy trades for the Lucky Contest. If I so wish, I can just leave it like that for as many times as I feel like EURJPY would keep on going up to actually achieve a good target for the day or just maybe one round or two rounds of it achieving a positive 10 pips in each round or I might even decide to close it in between when I feel that there is going to be a reversal. Alright let me test this out.

Alright, Yesterday or rather two days ago, I was... price was around here and I mistakenly entered the trade GBPNZD for a sell of which normally for this kind of trade I don't enter GBPNZD. So it went all the way up and right now it seems to be coming down but really I can't really trust this whether this would happen before the end of the day. I was actually on this position around 4th of here two days ago on the 4th position. I wanted to place a sell on GBPUSD but unfortunately it went all the way up, this is GBPUSD which was around here that time, It was actually around here to be exact. I placed a sell around here. Even if I had failed, I would have... because it was still around here by the next day which was yesterday but unfortunately I placed a sell on GBPNZD by mistake. Why that happened I don't know but it happened and "I can't blame the cat". You know so, unless I am actually a 'lucky' trader, I might not win this contest but that's how it goes. Sometimes you win some, sometimes you lose some, for the very best.

LiteForex* Best of the Best contest. Now we can have a look about, look at the performance of people over time . This is the account balance, we all start with account balance of $5000 and here right now we already have someone who is already on 300% extra. Once in a while actually, we do see such scenarios whereby traders generally all make money, as in a lot of money as well because of... let's say trend was just nice so a lot of people just rode on the wave of the strength and yeah a lot of money would be made. Saying you have the same fair level, fair leverage like everybody else so try to utilize the ones you are on at that moment.

Now there is this risk which is actually a function of several... of a particular calculation. Let's go there. So right now, this is... The account starts with a trade balance*of 5000, leverage of 1:400, you can't change that also the profitability to risk ratio this is... there is a formula for it but the most important part of it is that it should not have a high drawdown. You can go ahead and check it out on your own and then don't use a large lot size. A large lot size calculates the maximum deposit utilization rate and a maximum relative drawdown is based on the amount you actually dropped far down. That's for the drawdown. From the top here talk less of how far that you went down. That's for the drawdown. So in this case, this is a small drawdown compared to that of... small drawdown compared to where it came down ***.

This number 4 has a very high drawdown compared to the rest. So the highest is what is actually being used for drawdowns and your deposit utilization rate is the amount... the volume of the money you used, what percentage of the whole equity are you using? That means your drawdown keeps on increasing, that means your equity would also be reduced. Also that means your margin divided equity will be a little larger. So initially, if you actually had used a small margin in the first place you would not be in this kind of scenario.

In this kind of scenario, this contest is a contest that says use a low margin and try as much as possible to make profits because the overall winner is determined by the profit divided by the risk ratio. The remaining part of the risk ratio is just this formula. Where are you? Okay, this is it. But the most important part of the formula because this is the part on leverage and the amount lifespan those ones can't be changed. We have a 1 and a 1 there but on this one definitely we have a 1 which would give you a 3 at least. So try not to get higher than 5 otherwise you would be dropped out, that's for the risk.

So over here, the people on the top here, the topmost guy is having a risk of 5 but luckily for him his profitability is high but he should actually be very careful for him to avoid any drawdown at this and the date is almost completed. If I were this guy, I really would have stopped because the second guy next to me is also having a risk of 5 and his profitability is clearly not as high as mine. So the payment, the prizes are being given out to the first 5. This is actually a live sum given to you, you are being paid exactly this amount that is listed here and you can withdraw it or trade with it anytime. It's not even a credit, it is a withdrawable sum. Alright, so this also gives you an idea that this broker at this moment is also trying to encourage people to invest into… get themselves involved in a PAMM account. You know PAMM account that's a management account. So if you really see someone really performing very well on the contest here, that means this person really has a good chance of being a good money manager for investors. So previous contests you can also see the results. Profitability here, this is the risk here. So as much as possible try to get a low risk. So to achieve that, do not use more than 0.33 lots and you can use it like twice. Let me put… okay. The steps I took to actually achieve that are actually very very very long, so but the thing is on a account of $5000, do not use more than 0.33 lots if I am correct.

Alright, so this is… let me go back I actually made a calculation. This one ensures that you can't go more than a risk of 3 because it only just adds 1 to it. So this one and provided also your Stop Loss is like this. You can only use a total of 0.66 lots. This only encourages your margin limit is just this percentage meanwhile the commissions here… so this is the calculation. This is the deposit utilization rate. You don't use more than this between this range, your point here for maximum deposit utilization rate or rather let's say your margin usage would be within this range so as to use the lowest which is this range. This is the lot size actually that you would use rather. You can be chanced and actually redo the calculation for it. But you can use this amount twice, it lets you use only 1.5% of your account. Two of it, that would be 3% of your account but I think the Stop Loss would still work even at 30 pips but having the two losses, it still won't go more than that. But remember that this is just trying to achieve in between 0 and 4.99. So try not to use more than this one twice or you can use ot once if you are sure of the if it is just a single trade you want to enter. You can enter two different trades for different currency pairs based on this amount or lot size just to make sure you just are within a safe range that's why I'm telling you this right now.

So, we move on. So thi0 sis the lot size 0.33 you would use or let me write say 0.66 at once when your Stop Loss is within Stop Loss of 20 to 30 pips. Yeah thank you I saw that. Yeah, I am talking to you the listener.

Right now all other contests are out of the game but this one right now. Hopefully maybe one day, LiteForex might bring their live contest, they had this LiteForex Marathon one time ago and it was really nice, it was a one week contest. A lot of these brokers... actually with the release of this video on the net actually, a whole lot of brokers will show more interest in contests, a whole lot of participants would be involved, that means there would be a lot more competitions among the brokers for more candidates, for more traders to come over to their sites, show them bringing various manners and various patterns to their trading rules and the rest and so on. Also, the prizes will increase. It actually encourages everybody, it pays off everybody at the end of the day. So...

Chapter 5   -   How To Win – Strategy

Okay let's run this. Now this is let's say... let's leave this in the neighborhood and on this street we have been EURUSD. No no let me just... no just EUR. Okay let me just... let me start from the beginning. EUR, GBP, CHF, I usually start with the European currencies. Then USD, then CAD then, AUD, NZD, JPY so it's quite easy to put into memory. These are the base currencies you'll be trading normally basically and these are the ones that form all the whole 28 currency pairs. 1,2,3,4,5,6,7,8. So there is actually a correlation existing between them, so EUR* and CHF Swiss Franc. CHF, what's wrong with... okay CHF here. Alright let's call them twins and they live in the same house and then let's call these guys AUD, NZD and CAD. Let me say these guys are the twins and they have a brother which is CAD there and they actually live in the same house.

What just happened? Okay let's... and they live in the same house. And the, now what's the name, GDP was their brother but he was disowned. I guess all these issues that have been happening in Europe, the Resolution, the Brexit, you know actually made him a little bit distant from them so he was disowned and is living on his own in another apartment. Similarly we have other people on the block, we have USD and then we also have JPY. So, the real guys you should be looking out for are these guys that have correlations. These guys and these guys and these guys.

So, it is quite a way of balancing out say okay if EUR*... USDCAD is going up, AUDUSD* down and NZDUSD* down, they should be coming down. If AUDUSD and NZDUSD are going in the same direction, it sorts of like helps your trading system. Okay, if this one is going up, this one should be going up as well and this one should be going on depending on which currency pair they are on like for instance if you are saying AUDCHF and NZDCHF and CADCHF, they should actually should be going in the same direction, if one should be going up, the others should also be going up. That's when the strength... when they are... all three are showing their strength, their superiority over the Swiss Franc. But if you are having something like say AUDUSD, NZDUSD going up and then USDCAD should be coming down. I said should, I didn't say would take note because it is not all the time that this happens but there are sometimes when you notice this thing happening, it usually helps you balance out okay which... that means these gold currencies are the ones showing strength or if there is another case whereby USD is the one showing strength in the whole set and so on like that but right now it is quite easier for you to just to balance up since you still have a lot more currencies to show a particular strength then. You have a lot more of balanced view of this if you can view the issue of correlation happening.

For instance now, I said EUR and CHF are both apartment twins, they are having a good correlation here. So let me just show an example of... we have, let me just... okay look at this one keeps coming down and this one keeps coming up the same way. Of course, out of the two of them, one of them would be stronger, we can actually go ahead and check out EURCHF. One of them would definitely going to be stronger, it's really been wobbling this way today. Alright, I want to show you CADCHF and EURCAD. Now, take a look at this one coming all the way down and this one going all the way up. Remember we are still trying to say that the Canadian Dollar is the one that is showing strength because it is the base currency, it is showing strength all the way up, the Canadian Dollar is showing strength all the way down here. So and then over here, it just came down from the beginning of the day before it now turned up and then similarly, this one went up from the beginning of the day before it now came down.

There are some particular currencies that actually have exact almost exact correlations. These are the ones you want to want to take good note of. Let me do something similar on let me say… let's try it on the New Zealand Dollar too. That is EURNZD and NZDCHF yeah. Alright, put a blank profile, quite faster and easy that way. It went all the way up from the beginning of the day now coming down so this one should give you the reverse; all the way down, now going up. Can you see what I mean?

So if you can actually can get the trading system or the set of indicators that actually make up your trading system of course, that if it's saying something on one and it is also saying the exact same thing on the another, it gives you a chance of okay yeah good I will have a good chance of going ahead and taking this trade. Let me choose one, let's say EURNZD, let me use EURAUD good, my profile, I've got it right here, where are you? Going up coming down EURAUD, EURNZD going up, coming down. So now over here, I want to actually bring out AUDNZD.

Now the question is if both of them are going to showthat volume of strength per se, which of them you should actually go ahead with? Over here at the beginning of the day at the beginning of this time, the market was actually in favor of going up, coming down, then now it's actually sluggish in this place. So we really can't say which of these two was strong but later in the day, it as actually going up. So if you actually had had a trading system that actually told you that it was coming down and this one was also coming down later, which of them would you have gone for based on… it was around this time, this is 5 O'Clock, this was 5 O'Clock and between 8. So between that 5 and 8 let's see. This is 5 O'Clock on to towards 8 O'Clock.

You can see that over here throughout this period, AUDNZD had actually been showing strength. So if you are going to say EURAUD and EURNZD they are coming down, which of them would you go for? The one that shows much more strength would be able to pull the EUR much more downwards. So you are seeing in this case now, the Australian Dollar is showing much more strength. It pays you more to enter the EURAUD for the sell compared to the EURNZD. Now already before, we've already analyzed that these two of them had shown us they are going to come out moving in this particular direction but which of them would give us a better chance of more profits? Which is the one that actually moved much more at a time when it happened. This one was already sluggish before even making the move and it made a move much more coming down this way. Let me show you and moving around 111 pips whereby this one moved even les… we are supposed to even count it from… even lets go from the highest it even went to over here. Compare this 78 to 111.

So you can see what I mean. So you use a currency pair * that they are both associated with to see which one you would go for and use the relationship between themselves to know which of the two of them should be chosen. Let's see the case of… I mentioned EURCHF earlier on now over here EURCHF, EUR was strong here, this was on the 25th of June. Euro started being strong from here onwards. Okay let's see look for EURCAD… CADCHF and EURCAD on that 25th. Let's look at both of them moving, making a good move. Alright, this one and this one on that 25th, both of them didn't make a particular move let's say this one coming here, let me move towards another date. This one coming down this way… Yeah that's true, they have negative correlation. While I was expecting something different.

This one was supposed to go up, this one started going up here, this one started coming down here good. So now, which one of them would have more influence on the CAD. So CADCHF, so CAD was weak, the other currency was also supposed to be strong. Which of them should we go for, which of them would have been showing strength around this time of between 10,11,12 in that range that was before they all started making a really good move? So 10, 11, 12, so EURCHF around that 10, 11, 12. This is 10, 11, 12 per se around this region , I can't really say the particular one that would have been a good candidate for it, but by the time this 13 hour candle had closed, I would have been able to say "yeah, it had already been making a move towards the EUR been strong so that is why the EURCAD would have been a very good trade to have entered compared to the CADCHF. So the main thing is, find a currency pair* that they both actually would touch, a currency out of the remaining… they are all together 8, so if you are talking about 2 of them, you are talking about the remaining 6, talking about you will be able to find pairs for the remaining 6 and them comparing themselves, the two of them together like in this EUR and CHF, you will see which of them is actually showing strength over the other. That's the one you will now use in that kind of setup. I hope with this, I have been able to give you a little bit insight into trading systems though this is not a full course time where we can talk about trading systems in full but a later date, at a later time, we can really talk more about trading systems.

Okay now, we will be talking about trading systems, there is one aspect of trading systems I want to just mention though this is not majorly a trading system course but I will just show one or two things that can actually help your trading. So we have… by default you should know this which is that USDCHF and EURUSD they have a strong correlation, negative correlation actually because when EURUSD is coming down this way, USDCHF is going up. They are actually like inverse of one another. That one going up, going down there and this one going up this way and right now this one is just coming down and this one is just going up maybe because of the relationship of the Euro Zone that they have with themselves there. GBPUSD should be like that a long time ago but after the Brexit and all other major like the resolution all other major GBP news impact of those times, GBP at sometimes just decided to just take a totally different direction for itself but these two have always been like that but I will be explaining that showing the correlation in an excel sheet later on (done earlier*).

Let me show you an example. NZDUSD and AUDUSD, they also have a good positive correlation. This one going this way and this one going this way, coming down this way and also coming down this way and they also have a negative correlation to the USDCAD. This one's going up and then this one's coming down, coming down, this one like going up, going up. So they actually have a negative correlation to USDCAD and their correlation is actually because I guess because of the gold association these three have. The CAD, the AUD and the NZD.

Let me just bring up another example. Bring out the EURCAD this guy will give us space to work with. EURCAD and I'm looking for CADCHF yeah good. So EURCAD coming down this way then going up, going up this way and then going up this way, coming down, coming down. This is another one that had a negative correlation with themselves because of the Euro and the Swiss Franc there.

Now the concept of using a trading system… this correlation is to let you now okay, this is going to happen based on a similar thing happening on the other one on its correlate let me put it that way. So, if I have a trading system that says the EURCAD was going to come down here and the CADCHF was going to go up here at the same time, I would be ready to take either of the two or even the two. Another thing I can also use to know which of them I would want to take would be to actually bring up something about that actually links the two of them together which is the EURCHF in this case. So at this point where we are looking for which of them to... should we go buy on CADCHF or should we go sell on the EURCAD? Let's look at what EURCHF had been doing at that region. Throughout that period,... let's check the exact time. The exact time it happened was around 16:00 time, so if we go on to check out the 16:00 time around that period, around that region. So just before then, the EURO had actually been very very strong compared to the Swiss Franc The Euro has actually been showing much more strength. So if we are going to talk about the EURCAD here, which of them would the CAD be able to pull more? You pull more one on the one that actually is weaker. So since the Swiss Franc is the one that's weaker, so it is good to actually take the CADCHF for the buy run.

Another property that can change this is the fact that these currencies have different trading ranges* let me put it that from one to* the other. This is Analyze Currencies here, so this will give us the average daily range for each of these currencies. So we have EURCAD where are you? Somewhere here, so it has an average daily range of 92 pips and CADCHF has an average daily range of 47 pips. Remember earlier on, we were trying to say which of them would you have gone for, yes the EURCHF was actually going up this way meaning the Swiss Franc was weaker which would have been a better trade to enter over here meaning the CAD would easily have pull the Swiss Franc higher this way but also note that this one has a higher daily range CADCHF has a higher daily range than the CAD... sorry, EURCAD has a higher daily range that this one. So those two factors; the issue of the average daily and then the trend... the movement of those correlates at that period would determine which of those two you would go for or you go for the two of them depending on what your trading system says but the thing let your trading system say the same on both currency pairs at the same time.

How to go about using this in like say the contest Million Option contest which is the binary option contest we saw for InstaForex earlier on, just a matter of knowing which of the individual currencies is having a good strength at that particular time you can actually go ahead and now trade the ones that are close to it or all the ones that are... let me show you something like EURGBP which is going up, coming down and then... where are you, GBPCHF is coming down, going up going up which is the negative correlation.

So, if for instance now you want to trade the binary options contest, you know that there are 11 of them in all, so over here if you actually got a good trade for sell on this one and a good trade for buy on this one at this period, you actually could estimate okay that GBP is actually weak* on these two. At that period, you could actually go ahead and trade EURGBP going up for a certain period of time on the binary options contest and then GBPCHF coming down at that same time. You could actually go ahead and just trade all the GBP currencies at that same time. Let me check out GBPUSD at that time also, also coming down an then GBPJPY also coming down. There are a good number of times when these correlates happen, it usually happens across board on everywhere every that currency is showing up. So that's how you can go ahead and use it in trading the binary options contest as I mentioned before.

Okay one other thing about correlates I would like to show you, for instance now, something happened yesterday when the GBP was just coming down all the way down, now let me show you something about it in this chart alright, so GBP... now take note out these are the major three bars; 1, 2, 3. It happened everywhere. GBPAUD was coming down, it bounced off this trend line before coming back up. That was the same time it bounced off every... let me use these ones, that was the same time it bounced off but it was at the point when it bounced off this particular trend linen that it went back up. Okay, let me show you another one and then on GBPNZD it reached this trendline then bounced off and that was the same tie it bounced off everywhere else again, that was the second time it bounced off and then lastly you can actually see it bounced off on the trendline for GBPJPY. Take note that these things actually talk to themselves in terms of like each of them... everyone of them respecting the trendlines of the other ones especially these three 1, 2, 3.

Altogether these three are just... remember the correlation with gold that these NZD, the CAD and the AUD have with themselves. They respect one another's trendline, so it is actually a good thing to actually just put the trendlines on your chart as you can get to know which of them that actually has the possibility of actually going to be a reversal or at least even if there is going to be a minor reversal to at least say "okay, so if I has taken a buy, okay let me stop at this particular trendline, if I feel like taking a continuity*, let it be after that it had gotten to this trendline and then I can continue that way". I can't really predict or tell you exactly what your trading system should be but I just need to let you have those things in perspective in view that yes, these things happen for various reasons not just any how. They happen because some things are happening somewhere else maybe you are not actually being focused to check it out. So actually, my own trading system involves checking out a whole lot of currencies at the same time. That's why you see a whole of charts on my screen right here but this one's purely for the InstaForex contest.

Alright let's continue with this. I really believe I've given you more than enough information for now even for something that is not a basically trading system course, you've actually learnt a lot I'm sure. And next, we would be talking about funny strategies this 16 and 32, I will explain it right now . This can only be done for a contest like the Fighting or the Top10 contest which is just a matter of those contest that are just go ahead and win... get the highest balance. This is how you go about them. You enter a contest... remember in all the brokerages – in the demo contest - none of them allows you to have more than one account, so you can only have one account in a brokerage. So what you do in this case is to open 32 accounts. 32 or 16 accounts with different brokers, you open an account with 32 forex contest brokers or with 16 forex contest brokers and then what you do is you go all in. So let's say you are on 32 for the first time, you go all in, you go buy on half the 32, sell on half the 32, that will be you will be making a profit of 16 brokerages, a loss of 16 brokerages that is if you really have the time that is when you can do something like that, so at the same time on the same currency pair. So at the end of the day, half of it wins, half of it loses. So you would be left with 16 and next if you repeat that again, you will be left with 8 and then 4, 2 and finally you have 1 more.

Actually, I have never done this before because I don't really have the time anyway but this is a way for you to actually go all in and win. At the end of the day, you would have doubled at each step. So at the end of the day, you would have an account of you would have a multiple of 32 times whatever it is that the account started with. If you started with a $10,000 account, you would have $320,000 at the end of the day without thinking but some brokers - actually I have seen only just one which is IronFX - does not allow you do something like this. So if you are going to do this, please keep off IronFX because they won't be happy if you do something like this. But it is also possible if other brokers see that... the purpose of contest is show your best in terms of your quality.

One way you can go ahead to even discourage people from doing something like this is to go by the way of this LiteForex Best of the Best which is they want to... they actually evaluate you based on the lot sizes and the risk you used to win the contest. Under CashBackForex the contests mostly use that same method. The contests all of them mostly use the method of using... evaluating your risk. So something like this won't work on those kind of contests but if other contest brokers now are not happy with people using it because if lots of people use it, it really makes no sense at the end of the day because everybody is like everybody is just using a cheat mode or whatsoever but if they now say officially one of their rules is don't use this, then you don't use it with the broker but now you can still do it for some brokerages... for most brokerages anyway but if they say you shouldn't, then don't.

Don't think they can't actually discover the method people use because they go through the process of finding the winners, they check out how you trade, sometimes, I don't know if there is a way they can sense if you are using more than one account. It is like something I've heard about twice in several places that brokers can sense if you are using more than one Meta 4 platform. So well, you didn't design the software so the owners must have put some things in their PCs... in the software. Remember also that you can communicate from one Meta 4 platform to another Meta 4 platform, hope you know that. Amd right now, all Meta 4 platforms are all interconnected under the same roof, they all have the same major directory where you have... where the terminal exists.

So it is possible for your broker to really know if you have more than one Meta 4 platform. So you just make sure your broker is not against this kind of method, that's why I gave the method the name 16, 32 funny strategy anyway. Apart from that, it is actually legal for now but once it becomes illegal please don't bother yourself or if it becomes something most brokers are not allowing you do or they are discouraging you just like what LiteForex is doing by involving your risk in it then forget about. But for now,

Special tools I talked about

Chapter 6   -   My Contest Tools

Now over here I am going to hide some things from you for now because I don't want you to know with which and what settings I am using, more especially I don't want you to even know the settings that I am using so you can actually go ahead and discover your own settings.

I believe in this thing called law of diminishing returns, if you remember the book I actually mentioned the other time; How I made two million from the stock market by Nicolas Darvas, so if you go ahead and start using Nicolas Darvas' method today, you will discover that you will lose. That's one of the faults of letting everybody know what it is you are using so which is why when I am giving out these tools, I won't be putting the settings there or as a matter of fact I would release versions you would actually have settings that are way off what I use but I will give you suggestions on what to use. So don't even bother asking me because I won't tell you what I use but then using them the way you've been using your other indicators because they are actually… all of these things they are actually built up on normal indicators that you have by default on your chart so I will just give you example, give you an explanation on what each indicator is based on and from there you can now try to build up on that.

At this moment let's start to use the tools one by one, I showed you earlier this Analyze Currencies, just put it on the chart and then that's all. It will bring out the currencies and bring out the daily ranges for each of these currency pairs and the average - I think I used 10 days. May be the final edit of the work, I will allow you to change the daily average, how far you want to see the average daily range is covered.

Next we have the Contest Winner, I will like to show you that one last, because I would like to use that one along with some of the other ones but actually the one I use in all the contests I won, I use this very one. It is actual a very simple thing in the initial work when I did it. It's actually a… okay let's wait until when we get there.

Alright so let's put Money Flow Index, this is the normal Money Flow Index indicator, there is no big deal about it. It just shows the overbought levels and oversold levels, so it has the same settings. I use the default settings on all of indicators normally. I use default settings on all of the indicators so am not actually giving out my own settings so that's why I use default settings.

The reason I am not releasing out my own settings to the public is because if you remember this book, the book I mentioned earlier on, Nicolas Darvas' How I made two million from the stock market, now if you consider trying to use Nicolas Darvas method today, you will definitely lose money and that's because everybody got to know the method so there are sometimes you need to keep some things private to yourself. So and I am doing that for myself so, that's the Money Flow Index in action and let me remove this.

Alright so, let me put the, now another indicator* I use like that is the Relative Strength Index indicator is the same thing as this. The overbought levels and then next we have the… I will show you the Moving Average indicator, this is the Moving Average indicator, my default setting here is 14 but you can actually try to do other things like, this is the Simple Moving Average, for the Exponential, change it to 1, Simple… SMMA based on all the normal settings of the Moving Average just put them there. Anyone you want to use put the number. Your normal default is Applied to Close. You can chose to change to any of these other variables. You can do that just put in the corresponding number. You can even check out the Moving Average of another currency from another location. As in you can even be on USDCAD and check out the Moving Average of EURUSD. I can also do that for... alright right now we on the H1 chart, so if I go on to the... if I press 240 which is on the H4 chart. So the reason am not seeing this... alright let just update this chart for the H4 because it's quite far back. So wait for a moment and this is the H4 Moving Average so there it is. So for us to really be sure the current, this is the last price here, so let's check out the H4 on the same level. So it is updated right now, here it is on the same level. Alright, so the next one we will be talking about is... okay that will be the Crossover Stochastic. So this is the Stochastic Crossover*, this is for a sell here, sell, sell and a buy here. Ok this Stochastic Crossover Extreme, that's the Stochastic Crossover at the extreme levels... extreme levels yeah. Let me show you... too much noise.

Alright, this is Stochastic here, this is Stochastic Crossover for a buy at the extreme level. This is Stochastic Crossover for a sell at another extreme level in the overbought level.

This one never entered oversold here, this is overbought here and this is a sell, this is oversold here and this is a buy. Now I actually made this to be of this height just in case you want to apply it to for instance let me show you something over here. I want to drag it into here without it covering too much of your window there. You can actually increase the height to something, let's say 50, here it is. The height can actually go as high as 100 so but this is to let you... but I prefer to use it on a lower height here so that it can actually won't take much of... actually the color is actually bright enough for me to see it anytime I'm trading and it doesn't take too much space so that you can drag it into any other indicator and use it that same way.

And this is Stochastic Crossover, let me not bring it here, put it at another chart. Stochastic Crossover, so this shows Stochastic any time it makes a cross. This is a buy and this is a sell and so on. So you can decide to bring it over here so as to cross over here, here. So this is a crossover, this is a crossover, this is a crossover and so on like that.

So this is a crossover I said at extreme levels, Stochastic crossover at another extreme level. So this is an exact entry for a buy and this is an exact entry for a sell and so on like that. It depends how you want to use them. So this one, the previous candle had crossed so this is why this one is* the actually entry level for a buy.

Another thing you can use this one... another way you can use this one is, I think I almost did it in almost all of them, yea I did it in almost all of them , it's showing... you can actually draw out vertical lines or use arrows. You can put both at the same time These are arrows here and these are vertical lines, these are the entry point for a buy or a sell depending on what you want to trade so but remember, one other thing I will want to tell you is this, a buy doesn't always mean a buy and a sell let me rephrase it this way, a buy signal doesn't always mean a buy and a sell signal doesn't always mean a sell. Let me just put that in the air so you can use it to make meaning out of it may be today or any later date and lastly, let's talk about Stochastic level here. Okay, let me put it where these other ones are.

Stochastic level, so it shows the oversold levels and the overbought levels when the Stochastic is at oversold and the Stochastic is at overbought so there you go. So when the cross happens at that overbought level that's where this one comes up and so on. This is just... can help you just put up your Stochastic indicator, let me delete the indicator window here, let me delete this one. These are actually different. Deleting the indicator is different from deleting just the indicator that's there, so deleting indicator window will delete everything.

So let me bring out the MultiCurrency level here so there you go, Showing at overbought, showing at oversold levels. So it actually just gives... it helps your trading in the sense that it gives you a faster view of things without having to be unsure of whether it's there or not there. So if it has entered oversold it's there, so if it is no more in oversold just clear and blank.

Alright so lastly we will be talking about the Money Flow Index, sorry we've shown that, lastly we'll talk about the Contest Winner.

Alright I want to bring up the Contest Winner indicator. This indicator is actually a blend of two different indicators, it's a blend of the Stochastic indicator and Relative Strength Index*indicator. It's like filters out the various Stochastic crosses and brings a new and gives just drops a few of the values. By default, I open the arrows and the lines to come out and I can actually turn them off , that is true, ok I will do that.

So now, this is it, it just shows this one is for sell and this one is buy. There are also lines for buy, these ones are for buy and these ones are also for sell and this one is for sell also. So let me just show you the difference in that. Let me minimize this. So these ones, this magenta color and aqua color they are, they will come out there when you use opposite trading trade, this is false and these ones, the trade in trade, these ones are for the lime and the red color. So let me do this, we just want only this only these ones. It dependents on which of them you think is beneficial to your trading, I want to do the opposite rather. you can insert everything, your values are still the same. So it depends on those ones that will be beneficial to your trading, you can just insert everything, the values is still the same and there you go. Alright, it depends on what is going to be beneficial to your trading, those are those are the ones you actually go ahead to use.

So but let me just remove the arrows and let me show you trying to combine all of this in just a full almost like in a partial trading system. I don't want to show you trading systems, this course is not for trading systems but let just show you an example of it anyway.

Now this is not trying to create a complete trading system for you, but just to give you an idea of how to use this Contest Winner that I have here. Alright, so we have... I want to bring up the Stochastic Crossover. I will drag it inside here, this is how it... this is how I plan on using it. This is a buy, and it will only be as effective as long as it hasn't crossed over to a sell, this is Stochastic Crossover, so this is a buy, it will only be as effective as... so immediately this candle closes as a sell, starting from the open of this candle it will be of no more significance or use as in that is just how... let me just show you just particularly just for something like this right now.

So this is a buy in trend only as effective as until when it crosses down for a sell which is at the opening of this candle. This candle is the one that closed down as a sell. When this candle closes, at the open of this candle, this buy is finally shown as color red here. So, it is only as effective from here to this candle. From this candle here to here that's when this buy is effective and let's say this sell will be as effective as immediately it turns and gives a buy cross, it will be no more effective, it's only as effective as only on just throughout this period alone.

The entry of this Contest Winner indicator are just exactly the time when the candle happens which is the open of the candle it is on. So this one is a buy at this candle, a buy at his candle alright. So, let me just add a few more indicators just to give you an idea. Let me put it out on this other one. Remember that I told you that these two are correlates, though negative correlates, so let me move this Money Flow Index indicator and then put up the contest winner but without the arrows, without the arrows. Normally I wouldn't* have put the lines but just to make it clearer to you just for this lesson, you will see that and also I will put the crossover here.

I also have to use... I try to use the same settings that I use for this one Stochastic of it, 5,3,3. Also the same settings also for that of its crossover. Remember that it's the crossover of this one I am trying to do so immediately it crosses over, it is no more effective that's why I ***. Alright so we have EURCAD and CADCHF. So I'm using the buys and I'm using the sells, so these are buys, these are sells, this is also a sell, so a buy also, this one is a buy, I don't really care which color, buy is buy, I'm just using buy, I'm just using a... I'm not considering whether this is a "opposite trade in trade" you know for this like this one and the aqua, so alright. Now so here we go, I want to pick out a period whereby the two of them are saying the same thing at the same time. So if you are expecting a sell on this one, then you are looking forward to a buy on the CADCHF, so let me give you a scenario like that.

We have, EURCAD was saying sell here at exactly this time, and it stopped saying sell at this time 15:00 it started saying a sell at 13:00. CADCHF was on a buy at exactly that 13:00. Can you see that here. So I actually want you to have a look at it right there, so this is 13:00 candle and then this is 13:00 candle for a sell. At that 13:00, this one is giving a buy and this one is giving a sell, so this is a good trade to enter one or both of them. So one other thing you ought to use is if one is an entry, how do you go about the exit? Let me just go back showing you some other ones.

Stochastic level indicator showing overbought and oversold, let me increase the level, let me increase the level to 100 giving us overbought and oversold and then I will be bringing out the Money Flow Index and then the Relative Strength Index. I think I probably made the Money Flow Index twice. So that is the Relative Strength Index. So Stochastic level, ok alright, the height 100, Money Flow Index and then the Relative Strength Index. Money Flow Index, I brought out the wrong one earlier on and the Relative Strength Index.

You really don't need to bring out too many but the thing is when you are trying to create a trading system, you try to just see... you put out as many as you can for starters and then you stop it at... you remove the ones that are not useful thereafter.

Although this is not actually full trading course on a trading systems but when time comes I will tell you a lot more about it but just for now, for this process.

Alright continuing this, now over here these are 13:00 buy and we are taking our buy over here up to Stochastic level here, starting from here to when Stochastic level was at the overbought level. Now consider that on EURCAD at 13:00, it was this one ok ,13:00 hour sell. Now there wasn't really a chance for it to really come out to really make much move downwards this way but on CADCHF* was able to leave an overbought level around here so compare... you can take the two of them into consideration, one of them was overbought at a particular level on Stochastic and then this other one too didn't get to oversold on any of these three indicators but still after that it started going back up. It's really safe to exit on time based on the fact that you have already gotten profit without having to wait till the whole thing reverses back against you like on EURCAD. So the exit is based on what you are seeing here or just one of them saying extreme level. It's quite wise to do what exit around the same time for the other one too.

So this one was buy enough for this and this one was sell enough for this. Now we noticed that on these two there wasn't any extreme level that could have given an exit. This is just making try just to make a simple analysis of the whole thing so just like ok alright so go back into the back past again to see if more and more situations whereby its only… whereby this one will be the exit or this one or this one. Remember also that all these have various settings, you can reduce the value of the Money Flow Index but that will be RSI to give you better signals so that you can actually exit on time without having to be so long in the market. Stochastic also has extreme levels of 80 and 20, you can reduce those levels to give you better signals also to give you faster signals to exit on time. So I majorly use these guys just to exit trades so that I don't be in a trade just for just too long, it actually works that way. I know I have given out just too much to you, I think I will stop on that.

Alright let's just look at another example of how to use these things. Let's see another one, this is a sell-sell-buy-sell, alright let's see ok good, I think there is a buy here around the time, this is a 4:00 buy here and over here let's check out this one, there was a 4:00 sell. I'm not talking about they should be exact… they should happen at the same time but the trend should be effective for what I am saying comparing the two of them. This was a sell, this one but the sell would only be as effective as far as this bar. Let's have something bigger here. Alright, sorry I need to adjust to it on time. So this bar, this bar is as effective as it hasn't gotten to oversold, it hasn't crossed… Stochastic hasn't crossed down for sell. So at the close of this bar, this a cross down for a sell, meaning that at the open of this candle, it won't of any use to follow the trend on this and that's talking about specifically why I am trying to just give you a sample trading system, I am trying to just show you on this and then this one is sell at the opening of this candle and it actually the sell is going to be effective only on this candle because at the open of this next candle, it had given us a buy cross over here so right from here it won't be as effective. It would only be effective throughout the candle but luckily enough, it was also at a time when this one, this 4 O'Clock, also when this one was also on a buy. So at that time we take a buy on this one and a sell on this one.

So our target, take a look again, Stochastic 80-20 overbought here on this one and then CADCHF was over sold around here. So taking a sell here. Also what will be your stop loss? I won't give you a specific value for a Stop Loss because take a look at a possible range would possibly work out well for your Stop Loss you know, and then will be able to actually come down and hit the extreme level here and this other one too gave out an extreme level here.

So now do you carry it* out throughout the period whereby it's saying overbought and when it crosses down and leaves the overbought region? I am talking about this one so that when it is at the overbought region and when it leaves the overbought region or do you let it… you take it right immediately its overbought you exit? When it actually was overbought, and you closed at the candle of 8:00, that means you exit at exactly the open of 9:00 that's for EUROCAD. What about for CADCHF, it was oversold on 10:00 and that means by open of 11:00, you exit the trade. From here to here was around 6 pips there around and then but then remember if you were going to follow the same thing we did here that means you would have exited this CADCHF at the same time we exited the EURO/CAD that's if you were going to exit exactly when anyone of them gets to the extreme level. So you can actually get something else to like say when it gets to extreme level do I exit immediately the candle is… the buy is just there or should I wait a little bit to see if it's going to continue on that extreme level? Once you talk about how well, how long you should really carry on the ride. I won't give you anything hint as to that other than the fact that use whatever it is that you have been using before.

Similarly this Contest Winner indicator, use it based on the best Stochastic indicator settings you've been using before and the best RSI period you've been using before. This one actually forms a blend of those two, and tries to give you better values for entries so that happens to limit your risks and limiting exposures. This is it in action like this. Let me ust bring out another currency pair that have good correlation, this one and this one. So far so good you have seen it giving us something fantastic with just the Stochastic level indicator. Let's skip these two for now but on your own time, really go through the whole thing and go through everything and you will see how well you can actually get extreme levels whether it will work out for lower values of these ones for you to exit but so far so good you have been seeing this one happening one time here, happening another time giving us really good exits.

Alright, let's see the AUDUSD and NZDUSD, and this is USDCAD. Let's add USDCAD to this and let me give it a blank template. Alright so we have the Contest Winner and then let me remove the arrows and then on this one blank again. A lright let me just do this, Contest Winner there and we are talking about Stochastic Crossover there and then Stochastic level here so I can just go ahead and say save this template. You can give it any name, let me just do this, make it fast. So we want the same thing over here and the same thing over here, sorry, same thing over here. Okay to make this look better let's do this, we could just come around to move every other thing we don't need. You don't need to have so many on a chart. Remember actually this is a course, so I wanted to give you everything as much as I can. That's why you are seeing just too many of all these at once on my chart and moreso if you have too much of it on your chart, it will slow down your PC. It will slow down your chart and you don't want anything slow as far as trading is concerned. One thing you can do to make your chart work faster is to;

Number one: Disable the news, of course most of you are actually using various news websites. It will reduce every unnecessary usage and this one here: the maximum number of bars – you will make this one like… if it's the one you are working with not the one you are using for test, make this one shouldn't be more than 5000 and this one like 2000 so that you would be using this one to work as in every day trade but the ones you are actually putting at those extreme values are the ones that you probably use to do analysis because you want a whole lot of data to exist but if you are just using it just to trade, you don't need these high values otherwise it would only slow your PC or slow down your platform and you want fast executions at all times. So for now, on this one right now we are having just this, we are only putting on this, let's see if we can get something that will give us, no we don't need this but we need NZDUSD right. So let me redo that, very good. So let's look at where you can get ok, something happened right here, it picked up the same timings as before but by the time I refresh this, it should have its own, only its own. Like for instance its having the same lines it has on this.

So if you are using templates remember to always have its own timings its own bars alone showing up. So let's see for this day. These are the periods, let me remove the auto scroll, right so for this day, this is USDCAD remember USDCAD has negative correlation with these folks here, with these two folks here. So on this day, nothing yet, on this day none of them were actually correlating with it because by the time this one would have exited, this one was… let me just confirm, let me confirm. This is a buy on… okay they are negative correlates so you can't use the same buy on here and buy on here. This one's buy here ended at this time at 6 O'Clock and this one's buy was at what time? 5 O'Clock. So this would have been valid if the two of them were actually positive correlates because the buy was still in good trend, in good standing throughout these periods. So it would have been really good but unfortunately this is a negative correlate so you can't actually use this.

Alright so let's check this, not this day, okay there is another one here let's see. There was a buy here and there was a sell here. The sell started at 1 O'Clock and this buy was effective but it stopped at 1 o clock so by the time this one started, this one was no more in the buy credit the time this one entered for a sell this one was no more in a buy trend. Sorry, by the time this one entered and was going for a sell, this one's buy trend had finished. So there was really no trade based on that. Okay let's see, this is another one, this is another new day and let's go to the new day. This day is 5th, 5th, no this is 6th, I think I dragged it too much. Okay, this is 6th, 6th and this is 6th so let's see. There was a buy here, there was a buy here good, and then this one was a sell far off here. So it was just far off so we won't be using this but these two which are correlates are actually having a trade around the same time or around the same time thereabouts, yea it was actually the same time, this is 23:00 and this is 23:00 for a buy. Which of them was exited first? It was this one entered and got overbought at 9 O'Clock, this one got overbought at 10 O'Clock. So by 9 O'Clock over here, it formed a doji here, so you can actually… If you are going to use whichever got to their extreme level first, exit that time, don't care about any other thing else so which would have been just exit around… would be around 19 pips and this order would have been entry, here exit around here. Exit at 10*… no this is 20-21 pips thereabouts. So this is actually I would call it this is actually a good trade based on that scenario.

It's a training system but I won't tell you that this is the only trading system you can use this on because I actually have several trading systems I actually have on ground. As a matter of fact I even have… I will show you something right now or probably much later at the very end when I am going to be showing up on the screen. So, I will just show you about archiving your trading systems and making good use of them either for now or the future. So this is there and let's do one more.

Okay, let's see one more day on… this should be the 5th, this is the 5th, this is the 5th here. So from here to here, let's go on to the 5th here and go on to the 5th here. Alright, so obviously you can see something is happening right here and then over here also, you can definitely see something is about giving us a good trade here. So we could say from here this is… there is a buy here, there is a buy at 2 O'Clock but the buy was no more effective by 4 O'Clock so but this one we had a sell at 2 O'Clock so this buy… so this sell and this buy are correlates at a very good time. Alright, that's one and over here this is a buy at 5 O'Clock so this one was definitely of no use to this one so but this sell wasn'tas effective anymore by 5 O'Clock, this happened at 5 O'Clock. So by 5 O'Clock this buy was of no use to neither this one nor this one on that day. So this one and this one were both happening at a very good time. So we could actually take them to 2 O'Clock but this is a buy here and this is sell here, so a buy at this time. Remember we haven't fixed a stop loss, so go ahead, go through the past and see how far how much of … the how much it really would move to… for you to be able to say okay this is a particular Stop Loss you want to use. So that would give you a good average you can actually work with. So we going on to an extreme level here and then what about this one? This one is sell coming down to an extreme level here so this one which of them got to the extreme level first? This one got to an extreme level so at the close of this candle which was the open of 16:00 and this one got to an extreme level at 12:00 and exited at and let's say they got to the end of the extreme level at 13:00.

One other thing you can do is because you noticed that after a while, you will see that are you actually leaving too much on the table by just exiting just too early or you try and wait to see if both of them can get to the extreme level like say if you wait, you can wait until this one to 16:00 or if you waited untill 16:00, you would have gotten both of them at really good points to exit. You can actually make... one way you can do ii is this; you can say exit when both of them are at their same levels or if one of them reaches an extreme level and leaves that extreme level, that means that the other one would definitely won't probably get to that level again like this scenario. This one was at the extreme level here but it now left the overbought level thereafter. So you can say "okay I will hold on to this one until to see if this one will get to its own extreme level if it gets there instantly which is the open of this candle, I close or if one of them gets to the extreme level and tries to leave the extreme level meanwhile the second hasn't gotten to its own extreme level, then I will just exit this one and then this one both" but luckily in this scenario, the buy got to overbought level and the sell got to oversold level so it's quite easily wise to just exit here. So you actually use this method of exiting when both of them are in extreme levels or when one of them leaves the extreme level, you can actually get more pips over time just go through the past.

I believe I have given just too much, so until the next time when we are talking about full trading systems, we will be talking about a whole lot more, we would see more examples and see various trading systems in play. I use the same indicator... I prefer using this indicator a lot of times. Using it in so many scenarios and in various forms and I had to create this one from scratch just using basic indicators, Remember this is actually just Stochastic and RSI but filtered out and this is just Stochastic just trying to make it look I won't say cooler but just easier to use. So and this is Stochastic level at an overbought level.

So its quite easy just I just made this indicators just to make my life better. So I would... these are the items that I just went through with you just now, so even if you happen not to have gotten the tools before now, all these tools, all these ones I have shown you, you happened not to have gotten these tools before now but you need them, you can just come over to this site either you come over to my Facebook page – this is my company – so either you come to my Facebook page which is facebook.com/forexbyteemy and then in the shop you get to buy the tools and then if you need an upgrade, may be you want me to switch over the trading systems into an Expert Advisor for you, you can come over to the Service page and make a request for that. Similarly on gumroad, you can purchase the items* and also make a request for an upgrade to an Expert Advisor. Hopefully you would have created your trading system by then. You can do that also on here Fiverr fiverr.com/teemytee and gumroad.com/teemy facebook.com/forexbyteemy. So those are three places you can actually get me right now for now. If I add any other one in the future, I will let you know in my videos.

A d then I think this should be the book cover, front and back cover of the book and these are some of the other banners you will be seeing around. So these are the covers that will be out there.

So lastly we will be talking about the Scalping Multiterminal. Let me bring it out on a blank sheet. This is the Scalping Multiterminal, just put on a chart, remember to enable live trading especially if this one is off, enable live trading and then the inputs. It goes on to catch 10 pips here at every single movement. Here you enter a buy trade or a sell trade, the one I allow at the moment is what would be entered. Okay, I want ok let me put a sell trade for instance now, sell trade: true, then say okay then allow this. This will enter 10 trades in the direction of a sell.

Oopsie, now this is what I am talking about, I have it here on the GPBUSD chart, I actually keep it on the first one on the very left there and this not even a contest I should be using, I actually should be placing it on the InstaForex Lucky Trader contest because that the one I actually use to catch 10 pips.

Now, this is… there is a, there is a wrong calculation here, this actually should be 25 but before I make a sale (The Scalping Multiterminal Expert Advisor), I will put it… I will package it for a sale, I would have made the corrections to ensure that everything is compulsorily 10 pips to the net profits. So this one did not execute but this one was able to execute all five of it. I also want to let you know that the trading terminal starts from the left… starts updating data from the very left of the chart. So if you have too many here, that means it will really take a while for the price feed here but that's if your computer is evenslow anyway but if you have good internet connection, it really might not really but this is just a side note.

Alright, so I will be closing this one because it's wrong and let me still… okay no problem, I still want to show an example anyway, so this is it, this is it in action. Let me remove from one of them, so this is… Now, if for instance I want to keep on having sell until a particular level is reached, so I could say this here… I could say… let me… I want to say I am hoping that it would test this level again though I don't… am not… this is just an example, I'm not telling you you should do something like this or let's say you could draw a trendline – I think a trendline would be much better. *** than this. So I'm drawing a trendline from somewhere that is lower than this. So we have from here to here, good. So, if this one is going to come down towards this level here, I would say okay, I want it that at this level here – let me get the price around 1.1397, so when price reaches this level 1.1397, I don't want to execute any sell trades again which I will just say, come over here, edit properties, I will say sell target: 1.31… instead of going for 97, I will say 200 because I don't need to get the exact… I don't want to use… I don't like using the exact levels of trendlines. Remember it also tightens up as it is going up this way. So when price reaches this level, it will no more place a sell trade. That way, I can keep on catching 10 pips all this way till it gets to this level and leave it like that without even having to mind it. The first 10 pips would be caught here, another 10 pips, another 10 pips that is if my direction is really accurate and funny enough, this is actually leading into profit and it's even a contest and this is the Real Scalping contest hoping to get from 20… to 25,000 and this is like… this is the second week, so we have two more weeks to go. So there you have it and… let me close, let me just keep it. After the whole thing, I will have time to focus on it. So if you haven't gotten any of the tools and you wish to get them, get them at any of these three locations and between now and then I would have updated the pages you would be able to see what you want to buy or if you want to make an upgrade to change any of the tools to an EA, you can do that over there.

Chapter 7   -   Bonus Lecture

7,1 (In Closing)

Ok we've come towards the end of the course or lecture as it is, this is a bonus lecture. So next time, we talk about what we expect to see in the future which is the Multiple Sources of Trading Income I believe the traders will like to achieve because I believe one should have one source of income, one should be able to just spread out and have several coming your way so our next is How to Build Your Own Profitable Trading Strategy which is something that we all need as traders actually because there's no point in you just going ahead and trade and trade when there's really no consistent profits growing up. So for me, I won't say I am the best of best of trader yet so I'm working towards my own goals and I hope to really be the best or somewhere close to the best but the reason I am going for contests is to show I am the best. Alright, so I try to do better than what I am right now so but for others that want to be better than where they are, I believe this How to build Your Own Trading System will be of immense benefit to them all and with Multiple Sources of Trading Income, I believe that extra money won't hurt you anyways if you know what to do with it. So those are books you should look towards… video books like this in the future and make good profit from it.

Alright so these are my Facebook Groups, for now for this page, it has two groups under it. So the first one is for those that only just got the video book I believe you've really got more than enough of the value worth of your money from it. So, the only other thing you would need to just do is just upgrade to the Private Group. This Private Group is the one for those that actually bought the tools - the software tools which is more specifically the Contest Winner. These are the ones I will be giving them more focus because they are the ones that paid more so I'll be giving them more focus because I need to get them to really really win contest more so that someone that paid for the tools will be given much more focus to be sure that this person wins a contest over time. So, I'll be giving them much more information than this group here though of course I will be giving them the same information which is like "okay, a new contest, this is how you go ahead to win" but these guys will actually be able to correspond more with me as a group. So these guys are just a matter of listen; this is a listening group but this group will actually correspond with me and then we will keep on communicating. As a matter of fact, this group will be one of those that will determine the future of how I go ahead and progress in doing my site and doing my jobs because they will determine what I will… what next they want next and I will be sure to give it out to them when the time comes out.

There are lots of few bonuses here, anyways they paid for it and really, it's good to get our customers satisfied. And they will be the first to know about everything and I mean everything. I will have a discussion with them about what next steps to do and if they agree with me, that will be what we'll be

talking about.

So if you're trying to find me, you can actually find me on Facebook.com/forexbyteemy, Rehoboth Imaginators Co. Ltd my company name and my website which I'm yet to finish but you may send an email to me which is teemy@forexbyteemy, I probably might not see it for now until I'm through with this, I can't really do so much in terms of checking out emails here but if you really want to get across to me just send an email to me either on Facebook or you get to me on Fiverr or on Gumroad. So Gumroad.com/teemy on fiverr, it's teemytee (Fiverr.com/teemytee). Alright so I need to give you any addition of any new channel I am on, I will let you know in any of my future videos so for now this is where you can find me; here, here, here for later and here on Facebook. Probably just send me a message on facebook or fiverr for now. But on gumroad if you have any item to buy from me and you can't find the exact location you had* bought anything, just get across to me on gumroad or on Facebook on my shop here.

If it's a service, it is going to either be on here, here or here. Fiverr, Gumroad or on Facebook. Okay let's say for now just feel free to contact me on any channel that is available for you but preferably I prefer any one of these two. So in case anyone wants to actually meet me and fix a time to talk one-on-one with me and really take my full focus and attention, then you can actually book for space on the services page or you come around to the gumroad or to fiverr. You come around to check out on my consulting gig here and for an hour I give you one on one conversation with me and I'll be able to answer all your questions relating to trading, majorly forex actually and you would have my full attention during that period and you might just get what it is that you need that will make your trading analysis much more better that it currently is. It could even be a business opportunity you are thinking of going into but you feel you just need a little bit of advice to guide you along in decision making, yeah, feel free, I will talk to you about it. So at least you have paid for my time and I believe I should give you the fullness of the service and surely yes, I do like being paid for what I do and another thing is I also try to do the best for anything I'm being paid for. So, it's a win-win situation that way and it's a money you won't regret paying for.

And talking about extra sources of income, I would say that I'm actually taking in affiliates for my site… for my products on gumroad so I believe that this book going out there will actually encourage a lot of traders coming up into trade contests and you being a part of those that will encourage them to do so and

how to go ahead to really go ahead to win these contests and also some of the products I mentioned like Contest Winner and other indicators that will actually boost up your trading efficiency, you can get them on gumroad as well. You can actually get a good cut of the whole thing. I think that I'm putting it out at 40% yeah. At 40% extra commission for yourself which you can cash out every Friday in your paypal account and if you don't have a paypal account I believe by now you've been on internet for so long you should have a friend or two that have a paypal account that you can trust to easily send the money back to you on your behalf. But the thing is just keep on piling up your commission and every Friday, get ready to cash out from the commissions you make from the sales of my books or my products whatsoever. So this is just an extra tip for you and of course I believe extra money for you, extra money for me which at the same time saying thank you by giving you 40% for.

And for those of you that want me to manage accounts for you because some of you are already interested in doing that, I actually have my own demons which I have to overcome for now and between now and the end of the year, that's what I'll be focusing on and for that, I won't be trading on any managed account and I'm not even sure I will be trading on my own account for now but by January I will be fully focus to do that. But between now and then I will be doing this account management. I will actually be managing not a live account but a demo account which I will make open but of course you pay for it this time around. It's just for you to just see how well

I perform from your own end anywhere in the world so it's just a matter of giving me your login details, add it to maybe a Multiterminal, definitely it must be a Multiterminal for me to keep everything organized in one spot and from there you would see if you will see if it is worth it involving your account with me thereafter.

You can either do that on facebook or from gumroad. So there is fiverr, facebook and gumroad and from any of the sources, I get your account details and plotted in and it actually is for $10 a week or $30 a month or the Premium of $100 quarterly every 3 months. So, you actually have just from now to the end of the year which is just 6months. With an Investment sum of $200 you can really be sure of the performance of this trader that's really trying to hype himself to see how well a trader he is before you think of investing your thousands or millions or so there. So, I think I've really covered almost everything you need to know and then the next part of the course is just to meet me in the flesh.

7,2 (One for the Road)

Ok this is me at last, I want to congratulate you for making it to the end of this course, and I will also like to make a little round off for over the things we have covered, and then I will just give you little tips for the future alright. So we covered how brokers actually organize contests but another thing is that in any business we don't know who is losing money, at the end of the day, it's probably you are the target. Brokers actually lose money to you when you win contest and they give you money at the end of the day. They lose money because they are actually trying to make a promotion, get people to know about them and hopefully with that, traders can actually get to become traders at their brokerages. That's one.

Another thing is some actually involve themselves in a pro live contests as whereby traders can actually go ahead and trade on their platforms and then make money from their contest and usually money from live contest are more but it also pays the brokerages also because they also collect spread on each and every transaction that takes place during the live contest. It usually pays them that way and so… and brokers also do this promotion promos of giving calls to all those that have entered their contest in the past; their demo contest. So you won't be surprised if you enter a contest and you just see a broker's may be their rep department just calls you or gives you a call one day and ask you how far you liked their contest and how would you would like to open a live account with them.

So that's one of the plans of their investment. There is really no hidden thing about it, they just want to… they are just in the business just to make money and its quite easy, quite plain that way. There is no hidden agenda there, they want you to come around to their contest, yes enter, win if you can but at same time they also wishing for you to become a member of their brokerage in terms of being a trader there alright next.

Alright also for traders, we should realize that the money we make are the monies other people lose either intentionally or unintentionally, so one of the things you have to be concerned is that as far as I am concerned I will only just going to be interested in those that have actually made purchases from me or am interested in their wellbeing, these are the category of people I will be monitoring from henceforth and of course the more you are making any purchase from me, the more I am vested in actually seeing to it that you actually succeed as well.

If you want to start any business online, one of the things you should do is run a search to see if that business have been associated with any scam in the past to know whether or not you want to get yourself involve in that business. So taking a note of that business name and adding scam to it either on google or any of the search engines to see if that business has been involve in a scam. Yes you would find mine with one of such using my username that's teemy, adding scam to it and search it on google or whatever and then you will find one that is because I actually own a web hosting company and then one of my clients actually happened to have used a site as a bank site then, a fake bank site. So luckily enough, my own web hosting provider had actually blocked it on time but unfortunately the whois detail was already out and one of the scam phishing sites actually had picked it up. That's why you would see that record online and if you are actually scared that as far as dealing with me is concerned, I rather recommend at this point may be you should actually stop any association with me at this point you can go ahead and make a refund for whatever it is you have purchased and so you don't have to be scared about this person is going to take my money and run away with it. If you are that scared about me now, at this point I think you should click exit right now. And also this would be the first and the last time I am going to talk about this issue so that's how it goes because I actually recommend and I am telling you this myself so you can go ahead and make a research. If you feel confident or convinced to still deal with me in the future then go ahead, if no, let's exit like this.

Ok let's talk about the next thing on the line. In the future I will be making more and more products and then I plan on making my video productions better because this is actually the first major* one and I really tried actually, I actually put most of everything together alright and next thing is that ok, that my white board there so a whole lot of recordings are going to be better than this and if there are anything I actually missed out, please let me know and anything you feel would have been better for you to see in the future. But one thing is this, everything I'm telling you is going to be the truth in terms of these are things that actually happened so feel free to also ask questions as I said preferably on weekend except you have schedule appointment and meetings and you have been paying for that.

Another thing about you paying me for anything is that if it cost you money, I'm going to make sure that you actually get returns on what it is you pay me for in terms of that, you actually would wish that I take your money in the sense that I will give you good quality, not just anything not just any scrap. I have been in this business for like since 2005 that is 13 years now and I really know the ups and downs, I've really had a lot shortfalls even myself and even right now I'm actually doing something which is actually have people pay me to manage their demo accounts to let them see my account so people can see my trades as I place the trades on a daily, weekly and monthly basis so you can actually see me trade live to really verify some of my claims. Let me put it that way.

So back to the topic on ground, I actually plan making this book Multiple Sources of Trading Income. It's actually 21 or 22 or 26 sources of trading income but at the end of the day I couldn't find enough time to finish so I have been writing this for the past two years and at the end of the day something I stumbled upon a description on ForexFactory. The topic on ForexFactory that actually made me come out of my procrastination was something about verbal diarrhea whereby people were actually trying to say "okay I am better than you, you are better than me" that kind of contest that you know men and their ego do.

So they now said ok, let's have a contest and everybody put up a hundred dollars let's see what happens in this year 2018. And I went through the whole thing and was like since contest is going to be one of the source of trading I was actually going to write about, why don't I a strike of that alone and then put it up and then do this, so that's I successfully had got this done.

Now that actually I've done one thing actually and much more in a hurry to go ahead and make more actually and complete the whole other projects actually there are two other topics actually be able to complete one of the chapters of the big book actually, it's actually going to be video books also. I'm actually happy that I can actually go ahead and then begin to do works on the others and try to finish it up an then once it's out of course you will get to know about it since you guys are going to be in a place I can be able to locate you thereafter this recordings or rather after this first product.

Alright and what else again? Alright yeah, the two books you have How to Make Your Own Trading System, I will show you an example of one thing you shouldn't do with trading systems right now. And the next thing is about the other one 26 Sources of Trading Income. So they are on the other white board there but I won't show you. Alright so because I have already listed some of the pieces there but when its out no worries, you will see it all. I have already started working on it already. So now after this one, you can get to see more of my works and I hope you like this one actually also and if you don't like it let me know if there is anything you feel like I can actually add to the whole thing to make the whole stuff look better, please do let me know and then that's should be all. Thank you, bye bye.

Trading systems are… a lot of trading systems are buried inside those files there and by the time I am going to be talking about How to Build Your Own Trading Systems, I would have dusted them all and then teach you how to build trading systems from scratch, how to build out trading systems based on your personality. So I will actually go through various types; the ones that can be used for short terms and the ones that can be used for long terms and actually I have been coding EAs expert advisors for various clients just for the purpose of making their trading systems automated.

A lot of trading systems have actually passed through me and I've seen a lot and I actually can give you a few good ideas of what could work and what would not work and if you do feel like automating any trading system, just let me know and that is part of the services I do as well. You can contact me on both facebook or on fiverr mostly . If you have not gotten any of the other packages especially the software tools, those are the ones I actually built myself and I believe they are going to be of good use to you especially that Contest Winner, it's very very… it was actually something very very simple I'd made and I just discovered that it was just effective and then… there is this contest… there are some contest I didn't even mention about.

This contest in LiteForex from a $10,000 account by the next day, I was on 200,000 by the next day and that was the same tool I used but I couldn't come out to win that one because I had violated a rule which is don't let a trade* be lesser than two minutes. So unfortunately I just had to just bale out of that one and then there is also one contest I won, I actually came out 6th or so, the prize was $20 but the broker recommendation was that you have to deposit $500 to take your claim but really the mathematics really wasn't really working out well so I just didn't bother myself. And there was even another one also I won, someone's live account actually, but because it was someone's live account, I couldn't come out to claim that that's why you won't see it on my site or anywhere else *** like a mercenary service that way.

It was purely actually coincidental in the sense that I was managing his account and I could see that the broker had a contest and I told him to register that account for a contest and he did that and we won money that way alright. Also, I want to get somethings right with myself more like organizing my life between now and the end of the year so that some projects I can't handle right now I would be able to handle by then. That would include Account Managing, full scale Signal Service but for now I am just using this period between now and till the end of the year to test this out and that's why those that have actually gone ahead to pay more and got my tools actually, those ones can actually get to see those things. The signals service I will be giving out like an average of one trading signal per week so that you can just have a look at my progress between now and the end of the year. After that, by next year whatever you feel.

One question that might actually be difficult for you in answering is can you actually go out and win contest?

Well, when I started out, I believed I could win contest that was the first thing, believing in yourself that you can actually achieve this feat and at least win something. At least, the prizes were attractive on their own and it was free money anyway. Do I tried my best to do something especially when I started, I wasn't making so much in terms of winning a price but at least I was ranking high. So after a while I started studying what I could have done to make my performance better. So I started studying the winners and what they were doing the lot sizes they were using per trade and so on like that.

After a period of studying them and generalizing and get targets that could make one a winner, I started getting prizes little by little and I get could several at once and several together as part of let's say as trophies for myself. So you can also do it also. And if you believe that you need this may be extra blessing or extra grace ok good , if you are spiritual good, it's good, also that means it also shows you shouldn't the fearful of anybody speaking out negative statement against you because that the purpose of getting into religious activities so because it gives you a high chance of being over whatever opposing forces that is against you. So really you should believe in yourself also. That's the main thing, keep on trying until you achieve your main target.

I could also give you one other example that happened to me a long time ago, actually I had never been so cursed in my life like that and over something that I actually didn't do. Maybe today it's something I could have been guilty of anyway but as at then I was innocent of the whole thing and then but that was the period I got $800 as in $400 from two different contest and you can see the results from what I showed you and then yea, you also can achieve anything you want to achieve, you don't have to wait for best of the best conditions just do what you can at the time you can do it

I wish you all the very best.

Meet the Author

More about Teemy at https://forexbyteemy.com and https://facebook.com/forexbyteemy